De ...

Hope you aren't p!
shocked!

Making your mess your message

It could be what you

always wanted to know!

Lots of love,

Betsy x

Making your mess your message

Preparing your heart to see your dreams fulfilled

Betsy de Thierry

Published in Great Britain by Freedom Publishing Company

www.cccbathandbristol.com
Printed by Instant Publisher.com

Cover design by Immersive Projects
www. immersiveprojects.com

Copyright 2007 Betsy de Thierry. All rights reserved.
International Standard Book No (ISBN) 978-1-59872-956-6

Foreword

This book contains three quite clear sections which are planned to compliment each other. To read any one section without the others would be to miss the thrill of completing this journey.

The first two sections lead into the exciting concluding section three, 'The Message'. If you are aware of extreme vulnerability it would be wisest to read this middle section with a friend as a workbook. No matter what, chapters 8 and 9 need to be read and not missed out!

The book is written as a journey from denial into reality and through healing into victory and abundance. It is a life changing journey which shifts the ceilings on the potential locked up on the inside of people's hearts.

This book carries a message which enables us to break the ceilings over our life which stop us from seeing dreams fulfilled and being the person who we were created to be. People are unique and extraordinary, and each one of us can transform the mess in our lives to become a message of hope, victory and freedom to this world.

Are you frustrated because you know that you are not living life with confidence and freedom?

Do you notice the conflict between your vulnerable and professional self?

Do you want to live an influential life being the best that you can be, seeing your dreams fulfilled and changing the world?

Read on to begin a journey of revelation which leads to freedom, confidence and life in all its fullness.

With Thanks...

With so much thanks to all the people who have lived this journey with me.

My thanks especially to Andrew, my husband, friend and partner in the journey of dreams being released!

Thanks also to Suzanne King for her wisdom, patience and insight!

Thanks to those who helped with this book; to Sarah Cooper, Jo Dolby, Dannii Molyneux, Nat Callow, Caroline Gelderblom, Alison Fews and Jenelle Hultgren.

Thanks too to Robin Richmond and all at Immersive Projects for the book jacket, you guys are stars!

As ever this book is dedicated to my children, Josh, Ben and Jonah. May your messages turn the world upside down! X

Contents

Section 1
What Mess?

An introduction to the depths of our heart

Chapter 1

Preparing our heart to birth dreams

The waves were crashing against the sides of the sleek, elegant sports boat as the engine began its ascent into a gigantic roar as she took off, bouncing on the water, power pouring out of her highly polished body. With every thud and glide the kids screamed with sheer ecstasy as she cut the water with her impressive force. Their eyes were gleaming in amazement as we skimmed the top of each wave. No other boats were in sight. The water was ours. Miles and miles of sea ahead. We breathed in the air of freedom. The sun was streaming onto our faces like on a summer's day, yet this was accompanied by a cold, freshness which was exhilarating. Nothing could stop us as we powered through the white foam. Andrew looked at me grinning. Words were not sufficient. The world was ours. The world was as it should be. Perfect. We were unstoppable.

Our hearts felt truly alive. We felt the full force of freedom, the relief of peace, the energy of adventure. We were hungry for more. When you taste freedom and life, there is an insatiable desire to know more and to know the source of this powerful experience. Life, however, cannot be lived with momentary experiences of freedom. We know really that this is counterfeit freedom. Real freedom comes from the core of our being. We were created to know life in all its fullness. We were never meant to exist from day to day in grey, mediocre lives achieving some goals, knowing some joy, experiencing some satisfaction. Life is not a dress rehearsal, we get one shot at it and we need to squeeze all we can out of it! Our hearts need to be ready to conceive dreams and successes that we were designed to fulfil.

As we pass through life we collect memories of special moments like this boat story and we treasure them. We can ponder on these memories and find ourselves being saturated with warm emotions which can make us laugh aloud as we remember the times of fun and joy we have experienced. We also collect memories of less joyous experiences where we have felt failure and known shame, where the words of a friend have cut deeply into our hearts, where we have felt the loss of a loved one, or the pain of rejection or just a niggling sadness and disappointment with life. Each memory has been built into us and has helped form us into the person we are today. Each memory has influenced our reactions to people and events and has formed our attitudes and beliefs, even if we haven't wanted them to!

People are extraordinary. Each one of us is unique, and holds stories of hope, overcoming, longings, victories, fears and joys in the depth of our being. We are all destined to succeed in life and to know freedom, joy and adventure as we see dreams fulfilled.

I want us to go on a journey into the depths of the hearts of people, where dreams and silent pains lie side by side. As we journey together, I pray that this book unveils the mystery of a divine romance which I believe is in the foundation of time for each person who walks the earth. Please don't close your heart to the pages and let cynicism rob you of all that life can be, but allow hope and freedom to be breathed into your soul. Allow the one who is freedom to unlock the vaults of your heart and to bring revelation and healing to your longings.

Even as we have read these few lines, our hearts can react with strong defences built carefully to protect our vulnerability. When depths of feelings are spoken tenderly, it's easy for us to shrug it off, feel irritated and find ourselves proclaiming our strengths and achievements. We do not want to admit weakness and we have taught ourselves that it looks unattractive and unpleasant. We have often made silent vows to allow no one to see our weakness and vulnerability. We tell ourselves that we must remain strong and efficient in this pressurized existence.

We live in a world where we have mastered the art of pretending to be vulnerable whilst holding careful control of our feelings, passions, pains and the real issues that we hold close to our hearts. Vulnerability can often be looked down upon, (unless it is strategically played to advance credibility in gatherings of people who want to advance in relationships and play the part of having close friends while all the while scheming and moving strategically to paint a great picture of themselves!) Vulnerability is often looked upon as a hindrance that is for those who are struggling through life and have 'issues' that can't be managed or hidden easily. As a rule most of us often don't have time or energy to prioritise the exploration of the corners of our heart, it's too daunting and risky. We often don't see the need to take time to see restoration come to our depths while so many people are depending on us and with the demands of work or managing a home or children. What if we look and we find there are pains and hurts which cause us to feel weak and less in control. What could happen to our worlds?

The strength of feelings which lurk in the depths of us can be powerful and hold keys to our present situations. To deny or gloss over these pains and hurts merely causes us to live lives without true depth and with reactions or decisions which cause pain to us or the people in our world. To dwell on them with no hope of change is also counterproductive, but this is a journey where I want to introduce you to the one who can heal the brokenhearted and restore that which has been lost!

Ways that we numb our emotions

Sometimes we can subconsciously carry emotional pain around in the dungeons of our hearts which can actually add weight, pressure and dis-ease to our everyday life. Although invisible, and usually successfully managed, most people's buried emotions and experiences can destroy peace on their insides. These buried emotions can cause us to focus on anything which can numb the pain so that we can press it down and manage life more acceptably. Many of us have learnt to find solace in the behaviour that encourages us to numb our pain in work, food, family, perfectionism, a hobby, a relationship, drink or anything that helps us deny pain. These behaviour patterns are found to help us in the face of unmet longings, fears that are too uncontrollable to bear, and pain that seems to have no outlet. We'll often do anything to mask the feelings that lurk in the hidden recesses of our heart.

There are some opinions, beliefs, hopes and fears that we would be unhappy sharing with even a group of friends. The thoughts are too close to our hearts, too sensitive. Often they are treasured because they have been formed and moulded by past experiences. It's these which build us into the very person that we are, with all our unique reactions and values.

Our professional self and our vulnerable self

One way to help us grasp the concept of us holding hidden pain that affects our present is to see us by nature existing in two parts. Although I believe that we are actually made as three parts which are body, soul and spirit, here I am going to talk of the soul being in two parts. I shall refer to them as our professional self and our vulnerable self. Sometimes we can feel the conflict of them in our souls! There is our 'professional self' which is the person who we have to be when we work, manage a home, look after our children or care for our friends and relatives. When we live out of this side of us we are generally in control and organised. We feel good when things run smoothly. Our professional self has a carefully cultivated reputation with an image which we are happy to perform to. Then there is our inner self which is the vulnerable us, warts and all, where we hold our deep feelings. It's the part of us which hurts deeply when someone says something painful but hides while the professional self smiles and laughs confidently. Some people live more out of their vulnerable self and face everything from that viewpoint which causes them to get hurt easily and feel overwhelmed by the battles in their daily lives. Yet the story for many in this highly pressured society is one of separation from their vulnerable self. So many people today face the inability to connect with their true vulnerable self. These people can cognitively understand the feelings that others describe but these feelings primarily remain in their minds rather than the pit of their being due to a difficulty in truly feeling them.

Psychologists have used many different terms over the years to describe these two sides of our lives. The most common and obvious concept is of our conscious mind and our subconscious mind. The conscious mind works much like a computer programmer gathering information and integrating or storing it in the database. The subconscious mind stores information indiscriminately and can sometimes hold memory with emotions, sometimes memory without emotions and sometimes just emotion.

The professional self lives more in the realm of the conscious mind while giving little attention to the power of the subconscious. However, the decisions that we make, no matter how professional we are able to perform, are still largely influenced by our subconscious attitudes and reactions. This is why we need to give attention to and unpack some of the dysfunctions of our subconscious vulnerable self. Others would describe the divide in our souls as our present self and our inner child of the past. However, I believe that

15

our inner child can grow up and become healed and remain a vital part of who we are!

Think for a moment, how does my vulnerable self react to a hurtful comment? Can you picture him or her hiding, wincing or being angry while you carry on a normal conversation laughing? In a situation where you are nervous, like a job interview or asking someone for help, can you picture how your vulnerable self is reacting while your professional self is arguing internally that it's fine, that nothing bad is going to happen and you can handle it anyway?! Can you picture a situation where you felt shame? How did you handle it? Did you laugh it off while internally feeling pain and acute humiliation?

It can feel quite odd looking at ourselves in this way and it is sometimes difficult to verbalise this internal conflict. However, it can actually become quite a relief to see how restoration to our inner vulnerable self can create a more unified front with less emotional conflict between the two sides which in turn can lead to a greater confidence and ease in life!

A guy who has worked in positions of great responsibility dealing with millions of pounds, managing hundreds of employees said to me recently that this understanding of professional self and vulnerable self had changed his life. He always felt confident in his place of work and had a reputation for outstanding success in his highly paid job, yet he still faced a deep feeling of insecurity and anxiety in his internal life. The contrast made him feel a fraud until I explained that his professional self was clearly enjoying the challenges but his vulnerable self just needed some attention. He was ignoring his own deep needs and longings and living totally in his professional self where he was functioning similar to a highly tuned machine! His vulnerable self was beginning to scream loudly and was just beginning to interrupt his professional life enough for him to begin to realise that he hadn't given himself time to grieve over some of the losses that he had experienced in his life. These feelings were being locked out of his world but anxiety was beginning to leak gradually into it as his vulnerable self demanded space to feel.

A friend of mine who is a professional artist has had a revolution with her work as she has grasped this concept. She has concentrated primarily on painting fine, intricately detailed pictures of fruit, fossils, leaves and other objects of nature. Recently she has begun to concentrate on more abstract works full of colour and expression. I was totally overwhelmed when I saw her new work and responded with amazement as I stared at the canvases. I asked her what caused the changes. She replied with a grin, 'Well, in your words, I am now painting out of my vulnerable self!' The result is influencing and bringing life to hundreds of people as they are affected by her work.

There are stories after stories of people like this who have taken some time to look at their vulnerable selves and have an M.O.T of their heart. In doing so, they have had their lives transformed and experienced greater and greater degrees of freedom and 'life in all it's fullness.'

All human hearts ache

It's normal to know emotional pain and we need to acknowledge that all of our hearts ache and long for more freedom. Our professional self often doesn't have the time, emotional ability or desire to dwell on these views and yet it's that very need that can drive us into behaviour and addictions that can numb those feelings. It's those same feelings that can drive us into the arms of God. Denying the existence of our vulnerable selves for too long causes us to become hard and unfeeling, or we can become aware of a feeling of emptiness or void on our insides.

Each of us wrestles at times with feelings of hope, disappointment, shame and failure, insecurity and fear. No matter how much we try and escape these emotions, they will undoubtedly affect us at some point in the walk of life. It's a part of being alive. It's one thing for our professional selves to admit such feelings, but it's quite another thing for our vulnerable, inner selves to actually feel those feelings.

I'm sure that many people now reading this have decided that this book would be good for a friend of theirs as they don't have such issues! They are happy, successful and live a full and merry life! It does take effort to stare at our souls to allow any dysfunction to surface. It takes courage to look and stand and not run. It takes courage to feel the feelings and not busy ourselves, put on a mask, run to an addiction or lose ourselves in a sit-com. This journey is exactly that, a journey, and not a place where we stay for long. It starts with merely a recognition that the healing of our souls is a season that we need to take seriously, in order to unclutter those dark recesses of our hearts.

Why bother with this journey you may ask?

I believe that the place where we can really know life in 'all it's fullness', and healing rivers to our barren soul is the place of vulnerability in the presence of the lover of your soul, the divine romancer. You may not at this stage believe in the existence of this saviour or indeed have little hope left in your hearts of the goodness of a God who watches over you and cares about the details in your soul. I would love you to believe that there is a God waiting to bring healing, restoration and life to parts of your inner soul that currently lie undisturbed, barren, surging with silent pain and maybe bitterness and anger. All these emotions that lie buried and silent often powerfully dictate decisions and reactions in our everyday life. Jesus came to bring us life in all its fullness and healing of our vulnerable soul is a vital part of this promise!

Could I ask you to keep reading these pages to see if a spark of revelation could bring new life to your hungry and hurting soul. I have lived a journey myself where I have experienced the life changing power, love and healing in my own heart and in the hearts of so many others. It's an exciting journey into true freedom, where pain and fear are no longer the dominant yet hidden and controlled emotions, but instead where wholeness reigns and brings full satisfaction into the depths of our hearts.

Having a heart M.O.T and keeping a roar in your soul!

Some people are unsure of entering into a journey of seeing their own heart or vulnerable self restored and healed in case they become useless, unable to function properly or a depressive, self pitying wreck! We've all seen people who become obsessed with their emotions and we have looked on determined that we would never become so ridiculously pitiful! I believe, however, that the best way to see our hearts restored is to keep an overcoming attitude. To make a decision to have your heart 'M.O.T'ed' is a decision made from a position of strength and maturity. Many people are too afraid to even look at their hearts and they would rather avoid the truth and hide their vulnerable self. For those of us courageous enough to look and brave enough to make decisions to allow change, we need to actively seek to maintain an attitude of determination in order to see victory take root. Self pity, naval gazing and intense analysing only cause an increase in wounds and negative interactions! We don't want people to become 'I' centred as this can be a highly destructive experience, but we are encouraging people to take a little time to sort out some issues which can hurt others and cause pain to themselves whilst they remain undealt with.

We want to see a prosperous people raised up, who are determined, courageous and valiant in their fight to see their vulnerable selves whole and healthy. It's a journey which is about embracing the gentleness of healing and restoration while maintaining a roar in the core of our beings as we determine to overcome the negatives of past experiences and turn them into messages of hope and life!

Chapter 2

The power of atmospheres

'Man can will nothing unless he has first understood that he must count on no one but himself; that he is alone, abandoned on earth in the midst of his infinite responsibilities, without help, with no other aim than the one he sets himself, with no other destiny than the one he forges for himself on this earth.'

Jean-Paul Sartre French writer and Philosopher 1905-1980

'I have come to give you life in all its fullness.'
Jesus. The Bible John 10:10

Coming out from hiding.

It is in the core of our being to attempt to hide from the extent and power of the deep feelings of hurt, disappointment and pain. We don't want to focus on them, we want to hope that they will go away so we attempt at pushing them down, ignoring them and focusing on other more satisfying experiences. We're often not aware that we are hiding from our strong emotions because we have chosen to live in our professional self which functions happily and successfully most of the time despite what's going on in the depths of our hearts. It is easy to see however that as a nation we are holding deep pains and grief that desperately need a voice, with many people clearly feeling that they have to wait for a reason that society declares is valid in order to express them. This seems to be what has happened when various 'famous' people have died. When Princess Diana died the nation seemed to decree that it was a valid reason to express grief and pain and many people did just that. Everyone seemed to grieve! The grief that was expressed seemed to be extraordinary as many people were able to 'come out of hiding' and express some of the things in their hearts that had been hidden for so long.

At other times we have a tendency to hide our vulnerable self in order to cope with the depth of the feelings of pain, grief and vulnerability. Some people hide by physically withdrawing from the 'rat race', others hide by emotionally withdrawing and choosing to shut down their real feelings. Others hide by turning to food, drink, drugs, relationships, busyness, babies, a hobby or their image. Anything rather than face that neediness in their own soul. Many others have their feelings dampened with chemicals available on prescription to ensure emotional stability. Sometimes these comfort activities or medication can hide us successfully from hurt and pain but they are never completely sufficient to numb all feelings of need and vulnerability.

We are hiding because we are afraid. We are hiding because we are avoiding the process of dealing with the collective mass in the depth of our hearts. We are hiding hoping that we will never be exposed, or have our vulnerability seen unless it's controlled by us. We're hiding our vulnerable self because of shame. We feel shame that we even have needs and longings, failures and fears. It seems easier to deny these and live a busy, successful life if we can. The question that has to be raised is this; how long can these emotions be pushed down and bottled up for? We don't want to upset the apple cart but how long can the pile grow?

Although hiding our vulnerable selves and all that is hidden there is a natural reaction, the problem that we face is that our vulnerable self is more influential in our world than we might realize. Our vulnerable self is usually responsible for the majority of our reactions and attitudes and it therefore holds power on many of the decisions that we make. We like to believe that past hurts and pains have been carefully hidden and managed and don't influence and control our present lives. However, we can't run away from our past. It still has huge power in our present lives unless we are prepared to deal with it appropriately. Even if we work hard at our current life skills, we will still be actively influenced by our past wounds that lie festering in the depths of our being. Wounds that are undealt with can become infected and seep poison into our souls if we don't treat them in the necessary way. Although the poisoned heart is invisible to the human eye it can clearly be sensed by others. To have a wounded heart which is not tended to is to deny the invisible yet tangible and powerful consequence of a wound which lingers around the owner of that heart.

When we choose to want to see our vulnerable self restored and healed, we can be surprised at the deep feelings which lurk there which need answers. We muse that these feelings cannot afford to be let out, in case they ruin a normal life, unless there is a place of healing to go to. The good news is that there is a place of powerful healing for our emotions and hearts. We can come out of hiding to allow the negative emotions that are buried to be expressed in a safe place.

Hiding does not bring restoration. Being in denial of our vulnerable self only brings temporary emotional relief but long term confusion and pain.

Healing and freedom rather than surviving and coping

I want to tell you the good news that if we are prepared to walk through the pains and hurts in our lives we will be able to soar rather then crawl through life. We can fly above the storms, with strength in our being, not weighed down by the pains and unresolved hurt in our life. We can know life in our whole beings. We can know true freedom rather than counterfeit freedom.

I want to explain at this point the difference between self awareness and healing. We live in a society that encourages self awareness and we can find help relatively easily to further our understanding of ourselves with self help books and counselling. Self awareness certainly can bring integrity to our lives and peace and reassurance can come as we are enlightened, but it doesn't reduce the actual pain present in our hearts. I believe however that there is a way to know complete healing, where pain can diminish and new life can be found in places of even the deepest wound. Total freedom from past pain can be known. Sometimes there can remain scar tissue after a wound has been healed and this can cause tenderness when pressure is applied, but pain is no longer present. I believe that this freedom can only come in the presence of the Healer who is Jesus. I hope that this concept will be explained clearly in the pages of this book for those of you who currently don't walk in a relationship with Jesus.

If you are aware of a vulnerable self that could be hiding, a part of you that others don't know or see or a part of yourself that you have rejected as weak and irritating but which could affect your reactions, values and ability to soar through life then follow these pages as we unfold the journey of wholeness. This isn't about religion. This is about knowing completeness and wholeness in all areas of our mind, emotion, spirit and body as we were originally created to know. Since our creation, God planned for us to know peace, productivity, freedom, wholeness and rest in lives lived in relationship with Him.

Betach: hiding in total peace, boldness and confidence

Let me now take you into a place of safety and the place where healing can become a reality. The word 'hiding' takes on a totally different meaning in the Bible and reading some of its stories of real lives, we see how some people who knew a great deal of pain in difficult circumstances remained peaceful. In the book of Psalms in the Bible, a man called David uses words to describe the safety and comfort he found whilst praying and being in the presence of God. He tells us of how he knew he could remain confident and bold, trusting and peaceful despite the difficulties that he faced. He uses descriptions of God as 'the strong tower', 'the refuge', 'the 'hiding place' and similar analogies. He's a man who is in actual physical danger and is hiding from his enemies who want to kill him. As he hides in caves and shelters he remains confident and peaceful.

The other night I went to bed having spent an evening preparing to teach at a conference on the subject of hiding because of powerful feelings of shame. As I began to fall asleep I heard God whisper the word 'betach' to me. I wrote it down on some paper next to my bed figuring that it was a message from heaven and I would look up the meaning the next day. (I had had a lot of sleepless nights and felt quite happy to wait until the next day for once!) I went to the office the following day with eagerness and looked the word up in a Hebrew Dictionary. I had no idea if it was a Hebrew word, a Greek word or a made up word, so I tried Hebrew first!

The word 'betach' is defined in Strong's Hebrew dictionary as; 'a place of refuge, both the fact (security) and the feeling (trust); safety, assurance, boldly, without care, confidence, hope, safe, secure, surely (word no 983).

The similar word 'batach' is defined in Strong's Hebrew dictionary as: 'to run speedily and with haste for refuge, to trust, be confident or sure, be bold (confident, secure, sure) careless, put confidence, hope, trust (word no 982).

I was overwhelmed as I realized that God was waiting to bring revelation to us about the concept of hiding in a safe place with feelings of freedom and confidence and not fear. The word brings revelation on the feelings which can take precedence in the lives of those who are adopted as children of the source of life and the King of Kings. We can be people who hide in a safe and peaceful place whilst feeling total confidence. Here are some ways the word is used.

'The wicked flee when no one is pursuing but the righteous are as bold (betach) as a lion'.
Proverbs 28:1

'In God, whose word I praise, In God I have put my trust (betach).'   *Psalm 56:4*

'Then you would trust, because there is hope; and you would look around and rest securely (betach)'.   *Job 11:18*

There are many different Hebrew words for our English words 'trust' 'boldness' 'confidence', 'carefree' and 'refuge'. The word 'betach' however is a specific combination which is used to show the power of God's protection for our life and how we are to move into that position of safety by recognising and trusting in the fact of His powerful presence.

Whilst our professional self can either imagine coming to God or already does come to God feeling relatively confident, we can sometimes see that our vulnerable self is less logical. Sometimes our vulnerable self can be like a grumpy toddler with God, writhing and kicking in a corner on the floor or in His arms, feeling anger or too full of shame to go near Him. I remember holding my son Josh when he was two years old while he was having a full blown tantrum about his desire for something illogical when I felt God whisper to me with a big grin, 'You're like that with me sometimes!' I held him while he kicked, wriggled and shouted about the injustice of life and then suddenly stopped kicking and flopped into me, burying his head in my jumper while he cried and cried. As he cried he became all cuddly as he declared his love for me. He was expressing ambivalence as he voiced his total need for me as the one towards whom he had felt such anger and yet also the primary source of his comfort and security. So often we are not seeking comfort and healing from God because deep in our subconscious (or maybe not so deep?) we are actually angry, embarrassed or confused and so we are hiding from God when actually He is the very one who we need.

To 'betach' is to be so confident and trusting in God that both our vulnerable self and professional self are peaceful and bold no matter what circumstances occur in our lives. We feel protected because we know we are protected.

The concept of being protected by God in a 'strong tower' is not claiming that life will be lived with few difficulties and hard times. Indeed, the central story in the Bible in the Old Testament is of the people who follow God, the Israelites, who are given a land by him but are responsible for kicking out the inhabitants to complete the conquest. It's the journey of faith and doubt, confidence and fear, patience and grumbling. It's the story of people's individual and corporate walk with God. It's a story about overcoming difficulties.

Hiding in his love

To hide in the refuge of the King of Kings seems like an odd thing to say as we can't see God, let alone hide in Him! To hide in Him is really about having a revelation of His love and devotion to us as His children and learning to focus on that. God is described as the Lion of Judah, the Lord God Almighty, the Alpha and Omega, the Provider, the Healer, our Creator, the Redeemer, the Judge, the all consuming fire and our Father. There are hundreds of descriptions and names for the God of the Bible, and all shed light on His character and nature which can help us learn to trust Him as we begin to understand who He is. Throughout the Bible Gods love for His children is central to His character and is explained and recorded at every different point of history. We can learn to 'hide in Him' and find shelter from the storms and pains of life in His presence, when the depths of our beings are growing in a continuing revelation of His love for each one of us. To fully understand His love is a lifetime's journey, and to allow Him to reveal His tenderness and compassion towards us is vital and life bringing. One of the main purposes of this book is to help you understand how to hide in the love of God with boldness, confidence and peace, as this is a secret to a successful and influential life.

'You are my hiding place, you shall preserve me from trouble, You shall surround me with songs of deliverance'.   Psalm 32:7

'But let all who take refuge in you rejoice; let them sing praises forever. Protect them, so all who love your name may be filled with joy. For you bless the godly, O Lord, surrounding them with a shield of love'.
                              Psalm 5:11-12 (NLT)

In Psalm 91 it says:

'He who dwells in the shelter of the Most High dwells in the shadow of the Almighty. I will say of the Lord, He is my refuge, my God in whom I trust'.

To abide in the shelter of the Most High is a decision to recognise our need for His sheltering and protection. It's about us saying that we want to do life from a position of needing God and His love, power and presence. We run to His shelter by acknowledging our need for God. It's this need that draws us close to God, in fact so close that we're in His shadow! A place of total peace, protection, love, life and security is found by drawing close to God. Here, God can transform the mess in our hearts into a message that changes lives. It's in this place where we can know the source of life and freshness and vitality and let it be breathed into the core of our being.

Living in atmospheres

Hiding in God's refuge is all about thinking about and focusing on God and His atmosphere and presence of love, acceptance, power, wisdom, healing, intimacy and peace. The atmosphere of the presence of God as we 'run into that place of safety' is hugely significant and powerful. To 'batach' is to know the atmosphere of wholeness in your life. To 'betach' is to learn to focus and dwell on the presence of God and all that it brings. As we dwell on Him, we can begin to feel the relief of his love, peace, kindness, goodness, patience, power, mercy, compassion, joy and gentleness and feel surrounded by it.

There are verses in the Bible which describe the presence of God as being around us, in front of us, behind us, under us, above us, like a shield to us, like a banner, like a fire around us, a refuge, strong tower and many others. Goodness and mercy follow us, pleasure and favour surround us, power covers us, a shield protects us and He hides us in His fortress. As we think of, dwell or focus on that, we can feel confidence, safety, joy and peace no matter what circumstances are around us. It's an atmosphere that we can carry around with us as we live a normal life!

To understand His love further we usually have to get rid of some of the rubbish in our own minds and hearts which stop us from true understanding. We contain such huge amounts of junk in our hearts which will just be built upon further as we walk through life unless we choose to seek revelation and restoration. We need to grow in a desire to know truth and therefore see our dysfunctions clearly and then choose to allow God to de-power them! Most of our junk and dysfunction settled in our early years in situations, events, experiences and atmospheres that we lived in. There has been a great amount of research done which seems to draw clear conclusions that our childhood experiences cannot be divorced from our present identity and behaviour.

As we acknowledge this, we also ensure that we take full responsibility for our present lives and avoid at all costs a victim mentality fuelled by self pity. We look back briefly because we want to move forward with increased ferocity, determination, courage and success! We want to rid ourselves of any hindrances to our future which lurk in us!

The atmosphere as a child

Atmospheres are incredibly powerful. We are aware of them all the time, whether we are trying to find a pub to have a drink in, a flat to rent or a new job to take, we are actually assessing the atmosphere. We make many decisions based on the atmospheres that we feel. Each person we know also carries an atmosphere with them and we are either attracted to it or may find it relatively neutral.

34

We have also all met people whose atmosphere repels us but we are often unable to put into words the reasons for this!

The atmosphere that surrounded us as children has huge significance in our lives now and is often a cause of emotional dysfunction in us as adults. Many people are familiar with the psychological research that has been done which demonstrates how events in our childhood have enormous effects on our adult life if they have not been worked through. In today's society it is becoming an accepted part of the parenting process to recognise the long term significance of our actions and words as parents and other adults in a child's world. I believe, however, that the atmosphere in a child home is sometimes more key in explaining the wounds which adults can carry. Atmospheres are powerful and although many people can't remember any specific painful memories of their childhood they are aware of living in a negative atmosphere which has caused them to live with fears and unhelpful reactions. Others can remember the specifics of their childhood, but the atmosphere around the memories holds a key that unlocks some of their present pain.

Let me try and explain this further. For example in a standard middle class family unit where reputation and performance was highly prized and demonstrative emotions were discouraged, the atmosphere in the home could have been one of huge tension, anxiety, stress and striving despite the perceived view of others who saw the high achievements and the apparently calm environment. The adult who had lived in that environment could well still face a fear of failure and a dis-ease about his performance leading to anxiety and stress. He could still carry the belief that emotions are to be discouraged and his reputation holds the most significance in his search to be worthwhile.

In a home where the atmosphere was heavy with hopelessness, anxiety or anger a child could grow up with issues relating to fear. In a home where emotions were demonstrated with volatility the child learns to analyse reactions and atmospheres quickly in order to remain prepared. Is he or she coming home to a good day or a bad day? Is anger going to be expressed or love? In adulthood this person could still have to deal with fear as a primary issue in their present everyday life because powerless was felt so continually as a child. The child often felt deep guilt for not having the ability to change the atmosphere or they felt a weight of responsibility for being relied on to change the atmosphere. Often the adult continues to live in these roles with guilt and responsibility often weighing heavily on them. There are scenarios after scenarios to demonstrate the consequences of different childhood atmospheres.

Take a minute to remember walking up the path to your childhood home at about 6 years of age. Imagine opening the door. What emotions are heavy in the atmosphere? Is it happiness, carefree, joy, peace, liberty, relaxation? Or is there fear, anger, stress, striving, volatility, control, anxiety, tension, hyper fake happy, loneliness or emptiness?

As we recognise the emotions and feelings which were significant in our childhood we can see how God wants us to run into that perfect atmosphere of His presence to see restoration. It would be a pointless and possibly depressing exercise if we didn't have the place of healing to run to. There doesn't need to be panic or fear as we 'run confidently with boldness and sureness' to the presence of God to experience the healing power of God. Tell Him how you feel. Talk to Him normally and ask Him to heal your heart. We can know healing in our vulnerable self when we exchange the atmosphere that we experienced in our childhood homes which we have carried around with us, for the atmosphere of the presence of God.

For many of us we need to feel those feelings which we felt as children while we 'hide in His presence' because we need to grieve and receive healing and restoration for our souls. Jesus desires that we all live in a relationship with Him, where we give our lives to Him to lead. The place of surrendering our lives to His lordship is a place of total freedom and peace. We pray, (which is just talking to Him either out loud or in your head- you don't need to use weird religious words, just talk normally) and tell Him that we want Him in the centre of our lives. He then promises to never leave us or abandon us. He promises that the Holy Spirit will empower us and remain with us forever! So to 'run into His presence' really just means that we are deciding to hang out with Him, remember Him, dwell on Him, focus on Him in our lives. We can do that anywhere; sitting on our sofas, walking in the country, sitting in the kitchen, driving to work! Anywhere and anytime we can choose to sit in the atmosphere of the healer, the lover of our souls. It is such a great thing to do that David who wrote most of the Psalms, said this;

'One day spent in your house, this beautiful place of worship, beats thousands on Greek island beaches. I'd rather scrub floors in the house of my God than be an honoured guest in the palace of sin. All sunshine and sovereign is God, generous in gifts and glory. He doesn't scrimp with his travelling companions its smooth sailing all the way with God of the Angel Armies'
Psalm 84:10-12 The Message Bible

Let me say it again! We can know healing in our vulnerable selves if we exchange the atmosphere that we carry around with us from our childhood homes, for the atmosphere of the presence of God.

Understanding God's plan for our lives

If I bought a brand new car for my kids, had it waiting for them in the garage and gave them the keys, my giving would be complete. The ownership process is up to them. They could just be grateful for the keys and the thought behind the gift and yet never move outside to see the car. Hopefully however they would trust, be confident and bold to walk into the garage and take ownership of the new car. I would hope that they would not just sit in the car and feel contentment with the atmosphere of the garage as that would not do justice to the present. My hope as their parent is that they would drive the car onto the open road and experience all the power and potential that it holds. This is the same with us in our relationship with Jesus. On the cross Jesus made a way for us to know His love and life and because He has completed His purchase for us, the conclusion of the story is up to us. He has made a way for us to know His love and healing, wholeness, peace, confidence and boldness and He wants us to know all this in all its fullness. Will we fight to know all that He has purchased for us or will we just survive and do the best we can with the life that we lead? Will we decide to 'betach' and live in the atmosphere of love, hope, power, safety and carefreeness? Or will we succumb to this world's stress, anxiety and emotional pain?

In the next chapter I want to tell you two stories that are fundamental to this journey. They paint a picture of how God wants us to know Him as a father who can protect us, heal us, bring us peace and lead us through life without anxiety and fear but with confidence and boldness.

Chapter 3

The story of adoption - we need love

We were created to be loved. There are many needs deeply engraved into our hearts and our main resounding heart cry is to be wanted, loved and accepted. It's in the hearts of all of us men and women to be warmly embraced and nurtured by people who cherish and adore us from the moment we are born until we become independent. The love we still long for in adulthood is an untainted love. We want love that is not full of impure motives, masked rejection and conditions which we can never totally reach. We need a love which is not ashamed to be demonstrated and voiced. Surely a love which is silent and not reinforced with words and actions due to a fear of rejection or inability to express emotion only adds to the confusion in the hearts of humanity. A love which is verbalised but where the words are accompanied by abuse leads to pain and fear of 'love'. Our hearts long for acceptance, safety, belonging, security, significance, intimacy and simplicity.

Understanding love.

Love is such a misunderstood concept that even as you read this you may have found yourself saying 'I don't need love, it hurts me' or 'I don't need love, it controls me' or 'I don't need love, it messes me up.' This pain which can be sometimes associated with the word 'love' is due to the damage caused by people who say that they love us and yet wound our hearts either intentionally or as a consequence of their own undealt with emotional wounds.

Our English language can be quite a hindrance to our understanding of some concepts like love. In order to understand what the Bible says about love, it's important to look at the original Greek language it was written in. The main word which is used is 'phileo' which refers to the love of friends or siblings. It is sometimes translated 'brotherly affection' and it is an uncomplicated love which is the foundation of friendship where each person desires the other to blossom and succeed. Then there is 'agape'. This is a unique kind of love which is found only in God's unconditional, eternal, unchanging, powerful love. It's a love not based on feelings but demonstrated with actions.

The agape kind of love which breeds strength and confidence is described in a book in the Bible. 1 Corinthians 13 says:

'Love never gives up. Love cares more for others than for self. Love doesn't want what it doesn't have. Love doesn't strut, doesn't have a swelled head. Doesn't force itself on others, isn't always 'me first', doesn't fly off the handle, doesn't keep score of the sins of others, doesn't revel when others grovel, takes pleasure in the flowering of truth, puts up with anything, trusts God always, always looks for the best, never looks back, but keeps going to the end. Love never dies.' The Message Bible

This is the love which all of our hearts long for. Yet we live in a world full of hurting people where families are fragmenting, the divorce rate is sky high and loneliness is as common and as deadly as cancer. There is hope. The following stories demonstrate a message of love which is possibly beyond our own human experience and almost, but not quite, beyond our comprehension. It's the story of divine, perfect love.

A story of unconditional love

The first story that will help our subconscious to grasp this love, is centred on the lives of men. There are two brothers who live with their father and work hard on the family farm.

Each son carries his own unique desires, dreams and longings. One day the younger son decides that he has had enough of the simple life that he has always known and he wants to break free and experience the wider world. He asks his father for his inheritance in advance to finance his dream. His father's heart is broken as he looks fearfully at his young son with all his youthful desires and frustrations. He gives him the inheritance which is demanded and the son leaves to seek pleasure and excitement.

Immediately the son begins to squander this inheritance on pleasure and luxurious living, rebelling against the careful regime of his home. He flaunts his money enjoying the power that it gives him. He feels alive and increasingly despises everything about his father's home as he laughs at the seemingly small mindedness of his past lifestyle.

His mocking is silenced when famine strikes the land at the same time that his wealth dries up. For the first time since he left his father's house he realises that he has not been wise. He faces the fact that he has huge and resounding needs which are not being met. He is driven by desperation to work as a hired worker looking after pigs. The feelings of shame and extreme humiliation become his only company as he faces starvation and failure.

As he looks at his stark future, he is awakened to the revelation that his fathers hired help are treated with more dignity than he is currently facing. All the remains of rebellion, pride and independence seep out of him as he dreams of begging his father for a job working on the farm. The son knows that the only option left for him to stay alive would be humble repentance. His heart is ready. He recognises his immaturity and stupidity and is desperate to repent and acknowledge his foolishness. He knows that he has thrown away his inheritance and position in the household but would rather be paid a little to work as a hired help.

He begins the journey home pondering on all that he has lost. As he comes nearer to his father's home he sees a figure running towards him. It is his father, filled with compassion and love as he kisses and holds his son with relief and tenderness. The son verbalises his desperate repentance whilst still assuming that his father will make him pay due penance for his stupidity and foolishness. Yet his father shouts instructions to his servants to get the best clothes and best food ready for a party to celebrate the home coming of his son. He is amazed at his father's response. Surely he has misunderstood something? The father says to everyone,

'Quickly bring out the best robe and put it on him, and put a ring on his hand and sandals on his feet, and bring the fattened calf, kill it, and let us eat and celebrate; for this son of mine was dead and has come to life again; he was lost and has been found.'

Luke 15:22-24

What a surprise to the son! Not only was he forgiven but also restored to his position in the house with celebrations and demonstrative love!

This story is written to help us grasp the love that our heavenly father God has for each one of us. It's a love which is completely alien to most of our hearts. All of us have known rebellion and selfishness when we have lived life our own way with our own pleasures and cares in the centre. When we have discovered that this only leads to more pain and wounds many of us have not known where to turn. This story demonstrates that there is a safe place to run where we can know forgiveness, restoration, love, tenderness, healing and life. The safe place is the arms of God. The safe refuge and strong tower where we don't hide in fear and shame but stand confident and trusting in the love and mercy of a God who watches and longs for us.

A story of adoption and acceptance

The second story is a love story which starts as all good love stories do with the birth of a baby. It's not just any old story but the most perfect story of all time! It tells us of our purpose, identity and destiny as people who walk this earth.

The build up to the birth of a baby is a beautiful, cherished time laden with expectation, hopes and dreams of the new life that is being carried. The mother is energised with love, protection and passion for the life that's yet to be met skin to skin. The moment when a baby is born is the most extraordinary experience as the mother and baby finally lie together, each exhausted by its journey into the world. Here begins a brand new life full of love, wonder, new experiences and belonging.

This story starts differently. This baby entered the world without parents waiting with expectation and excitement. This baby was not welcomed and cuddled with joy and gratitude. This baby knew rejection, abandonment and isolation from the moment it entered the world. It's an inconvenience, an unplanned and unwelcome nuisance. The baby is born and immediately its needs are ignored. It's left unwashed, still attached to the cord which had been its source of life but now lies cold and lifeless. The baby is helpless and forgotten. It is unloved and abandoned in the cold night. The destiny is surely certain for this life. There seems to be no hope, future or possibility of a saviour walking past at this precise moment, for surely every second counts for this vulnerable little life as it lies without warmth, food or love.

'On the day that you were born your umbilical cord was not cut, you weren't bathed and cleaned up, you weren't rubbed with salt, you weren't wrapped in a baby blanket. No one cared a fig for you. No one did anything to care for you tenderly in these ways. You were thrown out into a vacant lot and left there,

dirty and unwashed – a newborn baby nobody wanted.'
Ezekiel 16:4-6 The Message Bible

The story then introduces a much needed hero. There is a prince who happens to walk past with a compassionate and tender heart. He pronounces that the baby should live and completely flourish. It's a beautiful and honourable act to rescue a baby. It's another commitment altogether to speak hope into its future. This is surely too good to be true? Could it just be cheap words that are thrown away with good wishes and a denial of the problems that the baby is born into? Could it be ignorance of the burden of the commitment needed to ensure fruitfulness?

'And then I came by. I saw you all miserable and bloody. Yes I said to you, lying there helpless and filthy, 'Live! Grow up like a plant in the field.'

As the story unfolds we can see that the prince doesn't walk away into pretence that he never saw the baby. He watches her grow from a distance and makes sure that she flourishes. The story implies that he financed and supported her in the royal house from a respectable distance. His commitment was beyond charity. It is love for a life that was desolate and alone. It is a determination to see her know no shame or dishonour.

'You grew up. You grew tall and matured as a woman, full breasted, with flowing hair. But

you were naked and vulnerable, fragile and exposed.'

The prince feels that she needs total completion in her life by marrying him. He rescued her, watched her grow up and made sure that she had all her needs met. He believes that if he could pour his love into her, her destiny would be secure.

'I came by and saw you, and saw that you were ready for love and a lover. I took care of you, dressed you and protected you. I promised you my love and entered into a covenant of marriage with you. I, God, the master, gave my word. You became mine. I gave you a good bath, washing off all that old blood, and anointed you with aromatic oils. I dressed you in a colourful gown and put leather sandals on your feet'

I wonder what your reaction to the story is. For the men who are reading the story, maybe you saw yourselves as the prince and pictured the woman as a phenomenal picture of beauty worth the effort of saving! Or maybe you just felt pity at the thought of a woman with such a desolate past? Or maybe you identified with the baby rejected and abandoned?

Many of the women who have been hurt by men may have felt concerned at the thought of a man rescuing the baby and then watching her, waiting to get what he wanted. This is merely a cultural interpretation on the story. Many of us have lost our innocence and find it hard to believe that a man could watch, love and wait without it being perverted or manipulative. Others may have identified with the story of desolation and would long for a similar conclusion. Others have hurts which speak of the futility and superficiality of human love and so believe that this is far from the conclusion of the story and wonder what trials await the couple.

The love which is shown in this story is one which is unfamiliar to our experiences and therefore due to our current culture causes suspicion to rise in us. No story can be so simple, there must be a twist. This wouldn't make a Hollywood film if this is as intriguing as it gets.

The story continues with a description of her new life, new role and all the consequences of this extraordinary love.

'I gave you linen blouses and a fashionable wardrobe of expensive clothing. I adorned you with jewellery. I placed bracelets on your wrists, fitted you with a necklace, emerald rings, sapphire earrings, and a diamond tiara. You were provided with everything precious and beautiful; with exquisite clothes and elegant food, garnished with honey and oil. You were absolutely stunning. You were a queen! You became world famous, a legendary beauty brought to perfection by my adornments.'

The woman becomes Queen and rules with her beloved husband. This is love unmeasured and undeserved. This is total extravagance demonstrated publicly without any shame or fear. This is complete adoption. It's a perfect ending to a perfect story which is not a fairy story reserved for childhood.

The story is found in Ezekiel 16:3-14 in the Bible.

Understanding God's love for us

The story is written to describe God's love for us, his creation. Each of us identifies in some way with the baby's rejection and abandonment even though most of us have never experienced such absolute horrors. We can see in our own hearts where we have felt desolate, alone, misunderstood and desperate to be known, loved and accepted.
The Bible explains that the saviour, Jesus came to rescue us and to restore us to being a confident, loved, secure, fulfilled and successful person who has no shame or dis-ease in ourselves.

Many people have heard the story that Jesus came to 'save us from our sins' which is an awesome truth, but stops short of the whole story. Here we can see that the conclusion of the story is far from a pitiful rescuing where the saviour leaves us to grow up always pitied, weak and pathetic. The good news is that Jesus plan is that we are restored from a place of desolation to living as the children of the King of Kings with all the love, authority, ability and destiny that that holds. Jesus came to enable us to grasp all that God is.

God wants us to run into a place where we can meditate on His love and enjoy the extent of it.

God doesn't want His creation struggling to find love and acceptance and hiding from the fear of rejection and failure. He doesn't want His children to have to hide their needs in behaviour patterns that numb the pain and shame of needing love. His love is enough to meet the deepest needs of human kind. His love is enough if we make the time to allow him to uncover our wrong thinking and misunderstandings and enable him to bring healing and new life. He wants us to know His love.

We will not be able to have complete revelation of our acceptance and identity until we have faced the wrong thinking and wounds that lurk in our hearts which disconnect us from truth. Just as someone who struggles with their self image is unable to accept a compliment, even if they manage on the outside to look accepting, similarly we can struggle to have true revelation of God's extraordinary love in the depths of our soul if we carry wounds and unresolved pain from past experiences.

Finding our need for love met

Unfortunately the story for most of the nation is that they are in total denial of their hurting heart and yet expend great energy desperately seeking to fill it with anything which numbs the feeling of a need for love. Most professional and respected people are getting all their love needs met in their career and identity. The feelings of respect, admiration, success and belonging can mask the deep needs for unconditional love. That's why some people struggle to retire or leave their work, because their identity is found in their role. Mothers are often obsessed with the success of their children in order to meet their own personal need for acceptance and success. Most of these mothers believe that they love their children with integrity when actually they are using them to meet their own needs and longings. People are eating more, watching more TV and drinking more to numb their need for agape love.

The consequence is that people are giving huge worth to these things which numb or mask their needs. The act of giving worth to something is called 'worship' and whilst many would say that they do worship at a shopping mall or football ground, others would defend that they are not worshipping themselves, their identity or reputation.

In the Bible Hosea describes what happens to people who give worship to things that mask their need for God and His love.

'Worshipping foreign gods has sapped their strength, but they don't even know it. Israel is like an old man with greying hair, unaware of how weak and old he has become. His arrogance testifies against him, yet he doesn't return to the lord his God or even try to find him. The people of Israel have become like silly, witless doves, first flying to Egypt and then to Assyria. They do not cry out to me with sincere hearts. Instead they sit on their couches and wail. They cut themselves, begging for crops and prosperity.'

Hosea 6:9,11,14 (N.L.T)

For many of us the pains, hurts and wounds in our hearts which motivate us to find worth in so many other things outside God seem too deep, raw or powerful to begin to work through. It seems easier to leave things where they are and not to disturb what peace and comfort we have. It would seem that the majority of people don't have the courage to work through all the pains inside of themselves to find healing and revelation. Most would rather for 'the devil they know rather then the devil they don't know.' However, the hurts, wounds and undealt with baggage held in our hearts have more influence over decisions we make and reactions and attitudes that we hold than we could realize. For those of us who walk in a relationship with God, we need to look God eye to eye in order to walk in the faith that releases the dreams which we long to see birthed. If our vulnerable self is hiding then no matter how confidently our professional self responds, we are not wholly walking in faith, because a part of us is hiding!

The good news is that we have a Father God who longs for us to know how much He loves us. He wants us to know how much He waits for our presence and enjoys our company! He is our creator who knows us already. He knows all that we have done, all that we long to do, every thought, struggle, desire and secret in our hearts. He still loves us and is devoted to us! He is committed to us knowing true freedom and wants to see us flourish! He can heal our hearts with His love so that we can become whole and able to live the lives that he planned for us. We can know His love and know the freedom, confidence and boldness of His presence as we 'betach'.

If you want to make your peace with God and start a relationship with Him being in the centre of your life, you could pray a prayer something like this:

Jesus,
I ask you to come into my life and forgive me
of living a life without you at the centre. I want
to walk with you every day and know you more
increasingly as a friend, saviour and lover of
my soul. Forgive me of all the stuff that I have
done which has hurt you and others and
cleanse me now as I make this new start. I
believe that you are the son of God who died
to give me this freedom and new life which I
now gladly receive!   Amen

There is a guy in the Bible called Paul who prayed this prayer for some people he wrote to who lived in a city called Ephesus. It's a prayer that we now pray for you:

'And I pray that Christ will be more and more at home in your hearts as you trust in Him. May your roots go down deep into the soil of Gods marvellous love. And may you have the power to understand, as all God's people should, how wide, how long, how high, and how deep His love really is. May you experience the love of Christ, though it is so great you will never fully understand it. Then you will be filled with the fullness of love and power that comes from God. Now glory be to God! By His mighty power at work within us, He is able to accomplish infinitely more than we would ever dare to ask or hope.'
Ephesians 3:17-20

The next few chapters look at some of the major wounds which lie in the depths of our hearts that need to be dealt with in order to live in freedom and know life in all its fullness. As I have said before, I believe that only God can heal us and bring us into complete freedom. Jesus came to bring us life, and life abundantly.

Greater is He

A song written by Nikki Fletcher

Greater is He who's in me
Greater are You than all the earth
My closest friend my saviour
So much more than I deserve

Who am I?
That you wash my feet?
The Prince of Heaven's blood
Shed for me

Who am I
That you called my name?
Nailed to a cross
Unfailing grace

Let my life bring you honour
Let my words bring You praise
Your great love is all I want Lord

My refuge, my shelter, my healer
and rest
Almighty Redeemer, Salvation and
Strength

From the Album 'Here we go'
© Christian City Church Oxford Falls 2007
Used with permission

Section 2
The Mess

Bringing transformation to the depths of our hearts...

Chapter 4

Defeating shame and insecurity

Shame and insecurity are strong and powerful reactions which can be crippling forces that disable us from successful relationships with ourselves and others. In this chapter we will see how this negative power can be defeated in our lives.

A while ago I felt God ask me to study how the word 'garment' is used in the Bible. I thought it was rather a strange word to study but I was curious to see what was going to be discovered as I waited to understand the significance of the word. As I began my research, I immediately realised how completely mistaken I had been. It was a treasure trove of revelation. I shall try and expound some of these revelations in the next chapters.

Garments are not just items of clothing which are worn as a practical measure to cover up your flesh or protect people from the weather. Garments in the Bible are symbolic of an inner reality. They are used to represent a spiritual or internal fact. The garments worn by a person are seen as an overflow of what is in the heart of that same person. I guess the closest similarity we have today is that of superman! When he puts on his 'kit', his whole nature changes as he becomes a new identity charged with power! We can know a transformation in our inner soul as we 'put on' new garments or spiritual suits! It does sound a little strange but follow this through and hopefully it will begin to make sense.

Several people in the crowds that chased Jesus knew healing from touching Jesus' garments, not from touching Him. The garments seemed to carry the same anointing and power as the internal spirit. In the Bible there are garments of shame, cursing, praise, filthy garments, holy garments and many others. It seems to be that in order to see our lives lived in the best way possible, we need to take notice of what garments are in our world, if they are the best ones we can have and how we wear them.

The garments which are written about in the Bible had huge significance in the lives of the people who wore them. The story of the prodigal son which I retold in the last chapter tells of how his father puts the best robe, a gold ring and sandals on his son in celebration about his return. The robe symbolises his re adoption into his family and his position as son. There would have been a spiritual shift when his robe was put on. The action wasn't merely a practical response to his physical needs but a symbol of a highly significant moment. The other story I retold in chapter 3 of the adoption of the abandoned baby speaks of the Prince 'spreading the corner of his garment over the young girl' which is a powerful symbol of his desire to protect, care and love her. She takes on a new identity and experience of life as soon as the garment covered her. She knew love.

The whole concept of garments or suits is only fully comprehended in context to the understanding of the word 'naked', which is not solely used in the Bible to describe a physical state of being. Nakedness implies an exposure and vulnerability of the soul as well as the body. It is a word used to describe our needs and frailty. The only answer to our nakedness is to find adequate coverings which protect our vulnerability.

The garments which I am referring to are spiritual, invisible garments which others can often perceive, although not see with the human eye. Although they cannot be seen with the natural eye, most people notice their existence in the person's interactions with others. A person of importance carries an 'air' of success and the whole atmosphere of a room can change as they enter it. This can be seen as a garment or suit of authority. A person who has a life where they have overcome difficult circumstances can be a source of reassurance to people who meet them even whilst never mentioning their story. They too, just carry an 'air' about them which can be seen as a garment or suit of victory.

Imagine being in a party and suddenly a hush begins to trickle through the crowds as people look around, questioning the change of atmosphere. You notice a guy casually entering the room with an air about him, which even he could be unaware of, yet which unintentionally has the power to alter people's view of the present. He has just sauntered in and yet the air that he carries affects the people around him. Some people know that he is the company director who they see only a few times a year, and here he is casually arriving, unannounced, interrupting their normal experience. Others are unaware of his job and his arrival but feel the discomfort in the atmosphere and react accordingly. People feel uncomfortable because he is a man who causes reactions and they question if all their normal interactions now need to be filtered to be appropriate. This same scenario can happen with any person who carries an air about them, with or without having a known position or label. As humans, we have the power to be atmosphere changers. All that we hold in our vulnerable self can change the atmosphere in the world around us.

Therefore we need to look at the concept of garments in order to break some negative feelings and mindsets which can put ceilings on all that we are meant to be.

Breaking the power of shame

The garment that I want to introduce in this chapter is the primary garment which we inadvertently choose to put on at the point of deciding to live with Jesus in the centre of our lives. It's a garment which breaks the power of shame and the fear of failure in our lives as we learn to 'put it on' and recognise it. It's called the garment of salvation and it dispels insecurity when we grasp its power because it changes our identity and position.

For many of us we experienced shame for the first time in our life because we somehow failed to do something in the way that our peers or family expected us to. Who has memories of letting a football team down by missing a goal or turning up to a school event or party wearing clothes that were laughed at as unfashionable, the wrong size or just wrong in some other way? Can you remember the feeling of wanting to cry or run away but knowing that that would cause you to lose even more face? That's the feeling of shame.

Many people walking the earth today feel confident and secure in their professional self but are weighed down by a feeling of failure and shame in their vulnerable self. Sometimes this shame has been a weight ever since some seemingly insignificant childhood experience. This is where the common behaviour pattern of hiding comes from. Everywhere we go there are withdrawn people who are fearful of others knowing their true self. They battle with intense feelings of disappointment with themselves and attempt to protect themselves from further rejection by remaining emotionally or physically withdrawn from others.

Many people also feel intense shame and fear at the thought of meeting with God face to face. Most can justify on a cognitive level how well they have lived their life, yet feel resounding guilt and shame in the depths of their being at the thought of God's eyes piercing into the motives and intentions of their heart. Shame can cripple people in their relationships with others and it can hinder a functional relationship with a God of grace.

Recently I spoke at a conference about the stronghold of shame. I had prepared a talk which was to last about thirty minutes and had allowed a further thirty minutes to pray for people who were struggling in this area. As I prayed that God would start to set people free and break the power that had held so many of them captive I began to realize the extent of what we were dealing with. The prayer time lasted a further three hours and the conference schedule had to be completely changed! Lunchtime was overlooked for many of us, as people's lives were being set free from a stronghold that had held them back from confidence and boldness for years and years. It was quite clear that this was a huge issue for many, many people.

Swapping the cloak of shame

It's important for us to understand the concept of shame better so that we can see total freedom in our lives. Shame is an emotion which is powerful and overwhelming. It is deeper and more intense than embarrassment. Shame makes a person feel so intensely overwhelmed that they want to have the ground open up and swallow them. It is a powerful enough emotion to make someone feel like they want to run away, hurt themselves or deaden their emotions in order to cope with the intensity of feelings which wash over them so suddenly. God wants to break the power of shame over our lives and lead us into a life of freedom where we can be confident in the face of experiences which seem to threaten our feelings of security and value. He wants us to be able to shrug these off as unfortunate mistakes rather than let them pierce into the core of who we are.

Shame is like a cloak which wraps people up in a crippling darkness as they try to numb their fear of rejection and failure. Often the shame becomes contempt at themselves because of their weakness and humanity. The shame makes them despise their own soul even further because they allowed themselves to get into that situation which exposed their weakness. Jesus came to break the power of shame which emotionally cripples his people.

A king called David, who wrote most of the Psalms in the Bible, wrote about this garment of salvation:

'I will sing for joy in God, explode in praise from deep in my soul! He dressed me up in a suit of salvation, he outfitted me in a robe of righteousness, as a bridegroom who puts on a tuxedo and a bride a jewelled tiara.'
Isaiah 61:10 The Message

God wants us to recognise our humanity and weakness and not be ashamed but rather run to him to be covered with a pure garment or suit of salvation which speaks of our identity as chosen, wanted, adopted and precious despite our humanity. This garment of salvation covers our vulnerability so that we no longer feel naked and exposed, but instead feel known and loved. The miserable cloak of shame needs to be taken off and replaced with a lightness and ease in our hearts where there has been discomfort and heaviness. The garment of salvation is a covering which permeates acceptance, purity, love and peace into the depths of our being. No longer do we have to be weighed down with the darkness and discomfort of shame. No matter what circumstances take place, we can stand secure and peaceful, knowing our identity is found as accepted, understood and loved by the creator. Shame can be a consequence of the longings of the heart. The main desires of our heart need to be acknowledged, and when they are not it can lead to shame. The first longing in our heart is the need to be valued as worthwhile and significant. The second is the desire for intimacy and security.

The longing to be worthwhile and significant

The desire to be found worthwhile and significant is a longing which is in the depths of every person's heart. As children we grow up hoping we are OK and hitting the mark. The hearts of little children need to hear over and over again that they are doing well. In the Bible it also speaks of how male and female were created in the beginning of time to 'subdue the earth' and so it is intrinsic for us to need to rule somewhere and somehow and therefore, know significance. The greatest fear that is lurking behind this longing is the fear of being a failure and experiencing disproval. It can be emotionally crippling to live in the fear that we're not ever good enough and not ever being validated as worthwhile. Any kind of failure then becomes more than a mistake or a practical problem; it becomes a judgement cry on our very existence. To feel that we have significance is the feeling that we know we are worthwhile and accepted and therefore we can deal confidently with times of failure and disapproval. In the context of already knowing significance, these failures don't then cause intense feelings to resound in our depths. We don't need to hear continually that we are doing well because we already know in the depths of our beings that we are just fine as we are. When we have a healthy feeling of significance we have a feeling of contentment about who we are. There are no anxieties and intense longings for acceptance and approval. When we allow God to heal our hearts, we can know this freedom.

I asked my husband if there was a time in his childhood when he experienced the power of shame while he was growing up and he recounted a story that many of us can relate to. He was House Captain at his school and was responsible for finding a team to compete in the school swimming gala. He was unable to find anyone to enter into a specific dive routine and he therefore knew, with a sinking feeling the inevitable consequence. He would have to do this specialized dive, in front of about three hundred people, himself. He knew that he was totally unable to do it, but also knew that he had no choice but to try. As he dived into the water with the most spectacular belly flop, he felt the power of shame hit him and decided the only way to deal with it was to keep swimming under water rather than face the looks and sounds of the crowd watching. He now laughs at the story, remembering the powerlessness of the moment and the stupidity of the school system but at the time it did nothing to help him in the search for approval and significance!

The longing for intimacy and security

The second core desire in our heart is the need for intimacy and security. As children growing up we want to know that we are accepted and valued and we need it communicated continually and consistently. We yearn to be sought after, cherished, wanted and adored. When we have not had these needs met, a fear of rejection can take root. This fear can cripple us and disable us from functional relationships of any kind. Many people have experienced a rejection overload and have had to find methods to cope with their wounds. When we face rejection from an early age and then face further experiences of rejection, we can either store up these wounds in our hearts and press them down into denial, or we can choose subconsciously to no longer feel pain. We can freeze out the possibility of the pain of rejection by either withdrawing emotionally or withdrawing physically. Ultimately, no matter how we deal with it, we will still feel a resounding longing in the depths of our hearts to be known and to know others closely. For many people who have struggled with rejection, they live with a heavy cloak of shame for needing or wanting intimacy with people and a shame for having a fear of rejection. God wants to heal us from the fear of rejection and the shame of having a need for intimacy. He wants to restore to us the ability to reach out to others with confidence and wisdom.

Facing the possibility that our hearts actually have these needs and longings can be a huge source of shame in itself. To admit that we have needs and longings means that we have to admit that we are vulnerable and human, and this can make us feel uncomfortable and awkward when we are used to being in control. We have often been brought up in an environment which has taught us to deny our intense feelings, squash them down and keep smiling. It's normal for a little child to be told to 'pull themselves together and stop crying' when they are expressing anger, frustration or sadness at something that causes them pain. We're often taught to cover up our emotions and vulnerability as being inappropriate expressions. This causes us to be confused about our own hearts and reactions. We feel embarrassed and anxious that someone may one day expose our humanity which would reveal our need and vulnerability. This insecurity in the core of who we are causes us to feel shame about our identity.

If we have been raised in an environment where emotions are suppressed and not freely expressed, they can end up being devalued in the mind of the child, who then believes that emotions are only for weak people. If a parent's emotional life dominated the childhood home, then very often the child would have grown accomplished in denying their own needs in order to help calm the needs of the hurting parent. The child can end up with a heavy feeling of guilt about having unmet needs or a suppressed emotional bank of negative feelings that still need to be expressed.

Very often people grow up feeling that there is something wrong with them somewhere. Often, this deep seated feeling is because they had to deny these needs and desires of the heart, and felt abnormal or weird as well as shame for having them.

If our emotional needs weren't met as a child, it's sometimes easier to feel shame for having them exist rather than feel anger about not having them met. Have you ever asked what's wrong with yourself? That can show a root of shame.

We learn to deny all the longings of our heart and the pain that we feel when they are not met. We can end up feeling guilty that our needs have not been met because of the confusion going on in our hearts. The consequence is a heavy feeling of shame. God wants to set us free from the crippling power of shame. We don't have to live this way any more!

Wearing the garment of salvation as a breakthrough power

The garment of salvation is actually a foundation point of our identity and security. A similar garment is first talked about in the story of creation when Adam and Eve disobeyed God's one rule and boundary by eating the fruit from the only tree that they were asked not to touch. They were tempted to eat the forbidden fruit and as soon as they succumbed, they felt the power of shame hit them. The Bible says that 'they knew they were naked'. They made for themselves coverings from leaves and hid from God who was walking in the garden in the cool of the night.

Can you imagine having spent every evening of your life walking in the most perfect, beautiful garden with your creator, the lover of your soul and the source of all wisdom. What questions would you ask? Can you imagine feeling such intense love, acceptance, and life in the core of your being? Can you imagine not knowing any sin, wound, pain, shame or anxiety? All you know is contentment and freedom. Then suddenly, after eating the forbidden fruit, you find yourself knowing intense shame and having to hide. Adam and Eve reacted the same way as we so often do when we face an intense feeling of need and vulnerability; they tried to sort it out themselves. However, the manmade attempt at overcoming shame and fear was insufficient as they still felt shame to the point of needing to hide, rather than run into the loving arms of the God whose company they had enjoyed since their creation. Their natural response was not repentance about their disobedience and rebellion, but independence and further rebellion. God gives them an opportunity to repent and then 'makes a covering of animal skin'. They are covered for the first time by the blood of what looks like the first animal sacrifice which acts as an atonement for the sin. From the foundation of time, God has prescribed that blood was the only method of paying for the forgiveness of sins committed. As sin is described as being anything which falls short of God's perfection, we all need to know how that debt can be paid.

In the Bible it says,

'Now we look inside, and what we see is that anyone united with the Messiah gets a fresh start, is created new. The old life is gone; a new life burgeons! Become friends with God; he's already a friend with you! How? You ask. In Christ. God put the wrong on him who never did anything wrong, so we could be put right with God'
The Message Bible 2 Corinthians 5:17,20,21

When God covers us with a garment of salvation, we can know the depths of freedom from shame and confidence in who we are, and confidence in Him understanding our souls. We can be totally known and totally loved by our creator. This takes the shame off us.

The garment speaks of our new identity as children of God, the relief of being adopted permanently by our creator and greatest fan. He scoops us up, restores us and sweeps away the darkness of shame. He breathes lightness into our souls and turns our face towards His as He looks us in the eye and speaks of our value and uniqueness.

In Psalm 3:3, God is called *'the one who lifts my head'*. Who has known the power of shame cause you to lower your eyes to the floor as you feel exposed and embarrassed? God comes, radiant with love for us and lifts our head and restores our confidence and internal strength with His piercing look of passion for us as his children. The cloak of shame is lifted from us and we feel the lightness as it is replaced by a pure white covering which permeates purity and wholeness into the depths of our being. We'll talk at the end of the chapter about how to put on this garment!

A garment that breaks the power of guilt

We are told to put on this garment in order to run into the presence of the creator of all, who emanates holiness, purity and all that is goodness. As we are, with all our failings and natural leaning towards selfishness and sin, we could never come even close to the presence of God, even though he is the lover of our souls. Our own sin stops us from knowing the life giving relationship which is the source of life, healing, and freedom. We'll never be able to get ourselves ready for God in our own strength. Nothing we can do will ever make us holy enough to enter the presence of God on our own, we need God! God longs for our presence. He wants to have a relationship with His created and walk through life with us, helping, guiding and restoring us. The only way to enter into the presence of perfection and holiness is to have a covering which is complete enough to cover the depths of our beings. It is Jesus' blood which makes a way for us to have a relationship with God because it acts as a covering which brings total cleansing to our inner soul. This brings a new confidence and boldness which enters our soul because we take on a new identity. The garment is a white robe which doesn't just cover our external state but permeates into the very core of our being. The Bible talks about the blood of Jesus washing our sins away. It's the blood from his death which brings us our freedom and now washes our sin away from us to bring us relief, a new start and an end to the weight of guilt and shame. In the last book of the Bible, the book of Revelation, it talks about this garment changing our status and identity:

'They have washed their robes and made them white in the blood of the lamb.'
Revelation 7:14

The lamb that is talked about here is the final sacrifice needed to make a way for us to be able to come boldly and with confidence to our father God.

Breaking the power of false guilt

The difference between guilt and shame is enormous. Guilt is a legitimate feeling where our hearts know that we have done something wrong. The feeling of guilt is a healthy plumb line to show us when we need to repent or apologise to someone. We need to know the feeling of guilt briefly as it is the voice of our conscience. We are, however, not meant to be weighed down by a heaviness of guilt as we are told that for those of us who have asked God for a garment of salvation, *'there is now no condemnation for those who are in Christ Jesus' (Romans 8:1).* We are now seen by God as being covered in Jesus' own purity and sinlessness. Jesus died that we might know freedom from guilt. His blood washes away our sin.

'For as high as the heavens are above the earth, so great is His loving kindness toward those who fear Him. As far as the east is from the west, so far has He removed our transgressions from us. Just as a father has compassion on His children, so the Lord has compassion on those who fear Him'
Psalm 103:11-13

(The word 'fear' here is not talking about being scared of God. It is referring to those who are respectful and in awe of Him. The word 'transgressions' means those things that we do which hurt others or God.)

Jesus wants us to know freedom, confidence, joy and release from guilt! It's good news for those of us that have asked Him to forgive us. There's now no need to feel shame that we need a saviour! We all do! If you know that you want to start a new life with Jesus, then why wait any longer?

__Making a decision that changes your future__

Why would you not want to know freedom from sin, guilt and shame? Wearing the garment of salvation means becoming a person with a new identity, as a child of the creator God who loves, cherishes and adores us. He understands our needs and weaknesses and doesn't pity us or devalue us, but rather lifts up our heads to know confidence, boldness and freedom from shame.

Why don't you pray now to see the cloak of shame taken off and the garment of salvation put on? As you do, it begins to smash a ceiling which has held you back from success for years. It's part of the pathway to wholeness and strength in your soul.

To put on the garment of salvation and take off the cloak of shame, just close your eyes and pray. If you have been weighed down with shame, insecurity or guilt then choose to ask God for revelation as you take off the cloak of shame and throw it away, stamp on it and reject it and all the feelings associated with it, from your life. Then ask God to help you to put on the garment of salvation. See yourself being covered in a white garment which permeates into your inner soul with healing, freedom, purity and love. It's not an imaginary game, its just picturing in our minds the reality of what God wants to do and paid the price to do. The Bible says we are *'transformed by the renewing of our mind' (Romans 12:12)*, and so we need to meditate on these concepts until we really grasp them in the depths of our soul.

You may find it helpful to pray this, or read it and use your own words!

Father God,
Thank you that you want me to know life in all its fullness. I no longer want to be weighed down by a feeling of shame in the core of my being. I now take that cloak of shame off me and see it thrown a million miles away. I now choose to accept your garment of salvation, and I put it on, lift my face to you and see you smiling at me. Thank you that you love me, have chosen me, adore me, value me, cherish me and know all the vulnerabilities, weaknesses and frailties of my heart and yet you don't despise me in any way. You want to breathe peace into my soul as you speak your words of love and acceptance that I long to hear.

Thank you Jesus that your blood washes away my sin and failure. I no longer want to live my way and I am sorry that I have done for so long. I want to live your way, wearing your power garments! The power of shame is smashed over my life. Thank you Jesus.
Amen

Chapter 5

The void in our hearts - Counterfeit Strength

When we watch small kids playing happily in the summer air, giggling and laughing as they wriggle around on the grass planning games and adventures, we can see a sense of freedom. Their minds are overflowing with mischief as they happily concoct ideas of how to squeeze every ounce of life out of their days of play. Hopefully they know little confusion or trauma, and innocence sparkles in their eyes. They look at adults with wonder, assuming that we too play hard and spend our hours at work plotting adventures of intrigue and mischief. All the insignificant details in our daily lives can become experiences of wonderment to a three year old. Planting a seed, washing the car with bubbly water, mopping the floor, lighting a fire or playing with saucepans which become imaginary space helmets, all become sources of thrill and adventure for small children who greet life with anticipation and wonder.

We were created to know life in all its fullness. We were created to find pleasure and a sense of deep satisfaction and joy in seeing the beauty of creation; the rolling green fields with crops of different colours, the hum of the city in the early morning as people rush to their different workplaces, the smell of coffee and fresh bread being baked, the squeal of the children playing in the playground. We were created to relish dinners with friends, the feeling of goals achieved at work, the birth of a baby, winning a game of golf, walking round an art exhibition with a friend, the freedom to express opinions and laugh with others over a drink at the ups and downs of life. We can be free to feel, to express what's going on in our hearts. We long to feel like we belong, we are loved, we are significant, successful, secure and happy which can cause the depths of our insides to feel truly alive and flourishing.

We were created to experience a vast range of powerful emotions with ease and freedom. They are each important to express the journey of our hearts. Each emotion was created by God, who knows what our hearts need to be able to do in order to know 'life in all its fullness'. In our current society, many of our emotions are misunderstood and many people who are growing older have an inability to fully express many of their appropriate feelings and therefore, they are unable to teach the next generation.

Strength and emotional maturity is seen as being able to remain relatively emotion*less*. It is seen as normal to live out of our professional selves and ignore or even despise having a vulnerable self. Many people have ignored their vulnerable self to the point of it being locked away totally. People are encouraged to 'pull themselves out of it' or 'have a break' if it looks like any negative emotion may be expressed. Not many people feel certain of what an appropriate emotional response is or what the definition of a normal and healthy emotional life is. It looks like we don't have time anymore for people to have emotions, feelings or indeed hearts, as we have high reaching goals and deadlines to meet. Emotions seem to get in the way and slow us down.

For many people, they live a life through their heads while their hearts lie hidden and afraid of vulnerability and intense emotion. We have become such a cognitive nation where reasoning and arguments form the core of most relationships. Our heart responses are becoming harder to listen to, as we subconsciously despise ourselves when we feel deep emotion. We can become afraid of being out of control or being inappropriate and therefore of facing failure. We have been taught to believe the lie that we need to shut down feelings of anger, frustration, pain, grief, loss and sadness. These feelings are often seen as belonging to the lesser species of society who can't quite control them or shut them down, and so need help. They are seen as pathetic creatures who won't fully succeed because they are so needy and volatile. Yet this is counterfeit strength. It is a method used to stay totally in control which actually locks up the heart and puts walls around it so that its vulnerability and feelings won't be exposed. There are many dysfunctional ways to deal with our intense emotions. Many find behaviour patterns to numb their pain, or they become emotionally dependant on others or they end up finding medication to stabilise the feelings which they don't feel able to appropriately handle.

Valid emotions

Emotional strength is found in a healthy heart which can germinate the seeds of dreams and visions. It is formed in a person who has learnt to handle emotions well. This does not mean shutting them off and becoming efficient and controlled, but rather that the fear of being vulnerable, weak, powerless, despised, misunderstood and pathetic has been dealt with so that normal order can be restored. The irony is that when people are afraid of their intense emotions, they begin to control them which often leads to such a high level of control that they actually end up losing control altogether because the emotions are shut down. Many people are now in a situation where they feel that they have little control over their emotions because they are so locked up. Their emotions have been frozen. They now struggle to experience normal reactions of anger, grief, sadness or pain. They can often feel them a little, or after a time of processing can begin to feel them to a degree, but usually the emotions are not natural and free. In times of extreme tragedy, many people with frozen emotions are shocked into responding for a short controlled period before they are shut down again. Tragedy validates their need for emotional expression in a way that most other circumstances don't seem to. It's similar to how we deal with physical illnesses. Flu and chest infections are seen as a valid reason for time off work or pity from colleagues and yet a heavy cold is seen as pathetic! We all know that a heavy cold can be awful and yet we too play with the system and find ourselves exaggerating our illnesses in order to avoid feelings of failure and weakness!

I spoke to a friend recently who has had revelation that her emotions in which she has taken too much control, need to be melted into normality again She currently realises that she has to deal with a backlog of reactions from events and words spoken several months earlier, as she has had to wait for her mind to process before her emotions were able to be released. She commented on this emotional backlog which leads her to feel blocked up and confused about the depths of her heart when she does try and process her feelings. It's hard for her to be spontaneous or speak from her heart in some situations because she has to first access it and think about it. She has begun a healing journey to melt her frozen emotions, starting with seeing her core beliefs change about despising vulnerability and apparent weakness!

The importance of having free emotions

For many people who have lost this freedom to feel a wide range of emotions, they have done so because deep down, they despise vulnerability and perceived weakness. If we hide our vulnerable self due to shame, it actually hinders our ability to make decisions, have healthy intimate relationships or even stand firm in faith enough to see territory taken in our worlds. In all that we do, our vulnerable self is usually more influential in decision making than our professional self, as it holds powerful reactions and the emotional response of experience. The heart, which is the centre of our vulnerable self, is described in Miriam-Websters Online dictionary as:

'One's innermost character, feelings or inclinations; the emotional or moral as distinguished from the intellectual'.

It also writes,
'The central or innermost part, the essential or most vital part of something'.

So if we are ignoring, despising, rejecting or just freezing out our vulnerable self, we are going to have to live with the consequences of having substantially less resource to draw on in times of decision and interaction. As a follower of Jesus who wants to see dreams and visions for the future realized, it is it difficult to see them fulfilled even if they have come straight from the heart of heaven, if your vulnerable self is hidden. All dreams need faith to see them become reality and faith needs to be rooted in the vulnerable self as well as the professional self. There has to be a lining up of the two for power to be released. Therefore, we need to see our hearts and vulnerable selves restored and healed to be the place of conception for success.

Reasons for switching off emotions

Very often children (especially boys) are bullied into switching off their emotions because they are told that being cool does not include emotional responses. Many guys have lost the ability to express much emotion except anger. For many people, this is the cause of sexual addiction as they only feel truly alive in this moment because they have lost contact with the rest of their vulnerable self which holds the emotions and memories. It is wrong for men to be told that they must learn to hide feelings of emotional pain and sadness in order to be a 'true' man. Many have been called names as they cried in public and therefore have been quick to decide not do cry again. When any of us make decisions at these points of trauma they can hold us into life long behavioural and emotional consequences. We call them 'inner vows.' We can break the power of these inner vows as we recognise their hold and pray for release.

Another category of people have watched friends or family being victimized and hurt, and therefore, have assumed that they are weak in some way. In this assumption decisions have been formed to ensure that they will never be seen as weak in case they too are victimized or hurt by seemingly stronger people.

Many others have simply been brought up in a family or school environment, where emotions were regarded as the expression of weak and pathetic types. This family or authority thinking can have great power in moulding our own beliefs. We too, can end up believing these lies and assuming that any feelings we have in our own hearts must be denied or despised so that we don't fail or become seen as pathetic.

Some have experienced such pain and trauma in their life that their emotional bank felt overloaded and subsequently, they shut down their ability to feel intense pain in order to survive.

God can heal people of frozen emotions and help them recover the ability to feel a healthy range of emotions. He says that he came to '*set the captive free*' (Isaiah 61:2) and the emotionally frozen person is one who is captive to living in a controlled and silent world where their real vulnerable self is rejected and despised. This is captivity where God wants to bring life and freedom.

Emotional immaturity

This doesn't give us licence for another expression of emotional immaturity where we have no understanding of what, where and when emotion is appropriate. It is vital that we are not led or ruled by our emotions but we must learn to allow them appropriate room to be expressed. We must be people who exercise self control over our emotions because this is a fruit of the Spirit. However, we can only exercise godly self control when we are no longer being ruled by fears and strongholds.

We need to understand what a feeling is, decide not to bury it, but accept it as a valid response and then learn to express it appropriately. Some emotions are easier than others to learn to express appropriately. Some seem to have a habit of spontaneously overwhelming us but God can teach us how to deal maturely with these emotions.

Different levels of frozen emotions

We are all unique and we have all reacted differently to experiences that we have had. Some of us are now facing the reality that there are several emotional reactions which we don't feel comfortable with and therefore where we hold a high degree of control. Maybe these emotions need to be melted and reformed to become a healthy part of our lives once again.

Other people will be recognising that they control their emotions to the extent that they are primarily shut off until they can be buried no longer. Often in this behaviour, the slightest frustration can cause a volcanic eruption of powerful emotions which can sometimes wrongly lead to the belief that emotions are best left unexpressed. God wants to reconnect you to the whole range of healthy emotional reactions which can be handled consistently and continually, rather than in occasional outbursts.

For some others of us, we will be aware that there are whole areas of emotion which are shut down and closed off. It could be that you have never known any different way of living and dealing with life. Maybe you feel that to have highly controlled emotions is the best way to live because it avoids having to face pain and feelings of powerlessness.

However, for some of you reading this you will recognise that you are facing a void inside of you which aches to know life and freedom. Jesus says that He is the 'resurrection and the life' and He wants to breathe life into that void and restore that which has been starved. Even the emotionally dead can know life again.

Jesus and David - men who expressed emotions

In the Bible we see that Jesus was comfortable expressing a great range of emotions. It is important that, at this stage, we recognise that Jesus wasn't some nightdress wearing wimp who taught about fluffy things to pander to people's desires. He was a strong man who was comfortable in a conflict, who had no fear of what others thought of Him and so was not afraid to be bold and confrontational in His interactions with others. He said many things which are shocking in the context of the culture of His times. He told the religious people who were greatly respected that they were like whitewashed tombs, a brood of vipers, unmarked graves, fools and blind guides. These are some hair raising comment to make. He was a man who was familiar with righteous anger. This means that He expressed anger at the things which makes God mad like the religious people teaching others about God when they didn't have a heart relationship themselves, and just wanted position and respect. Those issues made Him angry and He could express it in a healthy way!

He throws the tables over in anger in the temple as He proclaims that it is called a house of prayer and is not a place for people to financially cheat others as they sell overpriced items.

Jesus was also comfortable with crying in public. When His friend Lazarus had died he must have wept very freely because it records that the people around him said, 'Behold how He loved him'. Jesus wasn't ashamed to display His grief and sorrow publicly. Several times it is recorded that He cried. He also cried when He was overwhelmed with love for people as He looked at the city of Jerusalem. He was primarily known as compassionate and loving which the little children sensed enough to ask to be in His company.

David, the king who wrote most of the Psalms in the Bible and who was named by God as 'a man after his own heart', (1 Samuel 13:14) was also a man who was confident in his use of emotions. He wrote poetry and even killed bears with his own hands! He wasn't some pathetic guy who was seen as unmanly. He was victorious in many, many battles where thousands would crowd the streets singing about his power and triumph! He was comfortable expressing emotions and wrote expressing the weight of many of them. As he was being sought after to be killed by a threatened and jealous king, he declared:

'I am weary with my groaning; all night I make my bed swim; I drench my couch with my tears. My eye wastes away because of grief...'   *Psalm 6:6-7*

Now I'm not suggesting that we all start to write poetry to express emotion, but I am suggesting that we should not be afraid of intense emotion and that we seek a way to express it which is appropriate and helpful.

What happens to negative emotions that are not expressed?

Negative emotions are the result of pain and difficulties which need a voice. They are meant to be expressed in order to release the pain rather than let the pain mess up our heart. If they are not expressed it can cause our hearts to be polluted and poisoned with unresolved issues of pain, unforgiveness and hurt. To have pushed a difficult situation away from our current thoughts does not mean that it is dealt with. We were designed to process negative experiences until we reach a point of healing and settlement in our souls.

When we have emotions that are highly controlled it is often because we despise our vulnerable self, have rejected it and have made a decision not to express emotions that make us look weak. This means that as we look down into our hearts we feel a void. There is an emptiness where life should be flowing and pouring out from the core of our being. Many people voice concerns about feeling this lifeless core, a drifting emptiness despite circumstances.

God can take us on a journey where he restores to us the emotions that have been lost in order for life to spring up where there has been emptiness. The void in the vulnerable self will fill little by little as it comes to life with all the emotions which it carries. The main reason that people often don't want to go on that journey to freedom is the same reason that most people have subconsciously decided to allow their emotions to become frozen. Fear is the crippling force which holds people in captivity. Fear stops people being the person that they are meant to be.

Looking at the fears behind expressing emotion

The primary fear for most people in expressing their emotions is the fear of losing control and looking foolish. Many people have decided that it is ridiculous to be emotionally demonstrative and have subsequently associated emotions with fear in their minds. To express emotions, we need to rethink some of the lies which are running around our subconscious like a tape, or a pre recorded message. Some of those lies could be:

- To be vulnerable is to be weak and pathetic.
- To express emotion is to be vulnerable and exposed which could lead to being hurt or shamed.
- To express emotion is messy and uncontrollable.
- My vulnerable self and the emotions that I feel are an embarrassment which makes me hate myself and my weakness.
- People will reject me if they see me express emotion or see my vulnerable self.

These lies need to be recognised as unhelpful and untrue. It's important to acknowledge which ones are prevalent in our own lives in order to see freedom take place. We need to think about what truth is and allow it to permeate into our souls to replace the lies with truth. Here are some helpful sentences to think about!

- Our vulnerable self is beautiful in its fragility and perceived chaos.
- Having hurts, wounds and pain is not a sign of weakness but a sign of being alive.
- My emotions are helpful to me in the process of life and are not to be despised.
- I must not reject my vulnerable self as it is precious and a vital part of my life.
- Being vulnerable and expressing emotion does not necessarily mean that I will be controlled, walked on, despised, or misunderstood.
- Being misunderstood or rejected is not the worst thing in the world as I have a God who loves me, and I can see Him heal my heart.

As you begin your journey of melting your emotions and getting in touch with your vulnerable self and all that it holds, please don't panic if all the emotions initially seem to be negative. As these emotions have room to flow, more positive feelings will eventually follow. Be consistent in spending time asking God to reveal his love and melt your heart.

Don't get into a blame shifting, victim mentality way of thinking and God will help you learn to express feelings appropriately.

Many of these fears and lies are connected to the primary fear of rejection which we will look at in the next chapter in more depth.

Let's be people who allow God to melt our hearts to life again, who are not afraid of our own depths and wounds but are prepared to see our heart become that place for the conception of success. Let's become people who have healthy emotional responses and can therefore, deal appropriately with difficult circumstances which occur without our hearts hardening. Let's become people who know balance and maturity in our emotions and who know where, when, how and what to express at all times.

If you know that you need to go on a journey to release your emotions and become emotionally healthy and whole, then you may find it helpful to pray something like this:

Jesus I thank you that you love me as I am. I repent for believing the lie that says I have to be in control of my emotions because it seems pathetic to demonstrate my pain externally. Where I have despised and rejected myself and my weakness, I am sorry and want to now allow my vulnerable self to express feelings and pains. I want to now speak freedom to my vulnerable self to feel anger, sadness, upset and pain. I trust you God, that you will hold me, be my sufficient one, and help me as I face these emotions. I trust you God that I will not be overwhelmed or powerless as I feel how my vulnerable self feels. I break the power that fear has had over my life in the name of Jesus and make a choice not let my life be ruled by this stronghold from this moment on. Help me Jesus as I hold onto you, walking into freedom from fear, knowing that I am loved by you and all the depths of pain hidden in my heart can be healed.

I trust you now as I allow you into my vulnerable self to breathe life where there has been death, and healing where there has been pain.
Amen

Chapter 6

Awaking the hero inside of us
Breaking the power of fear

'Courage is resistance to fear, mastery of fear- not absence of fear'
                    Mark Twain 1835-1910

'Perfect love casts out fear'.
                    1 John 4:18 The Bible

His head droops to one side in exhaustion, his face pensive, weary, yet revealing a mild glimmer of relief as he walks steadily, his every step seeming to cause pain, toward his home. He's made it. The brown, muddy blood spattered on his coat looked more like stains of play than war.

The hero has come home. There are no trumpets sounding or crowds cheering the victory. It's a silent return, where few notice his arrival. However, the battle was indeed won and it's a fact that can't be denied. He knows. The memories are held inside his head, his heart aching with emotions which need to be released. He has overcome. He knows the relief of victory, the thrill of defeating the enemy. Fear was felt, faced and overcome. Fear was smashed and victory awarded. The cloak of victory is now his, worn with a feeling of achievement and satisfaction as territory has been taken. The battle is over.

We too, have a cloak of victory to wear which can see fear defeated and the hero in us let loose to take increasing conquests. We are not created to cower under the influence of fear, and get to the end of our lives with regret because of risks that were avoided, relationships that were never healed, joy that was only an occasional experience and dreams that were never birthed. We need to actively seek to find where fear is holding us back, and choose to root it out of our lives and live in an atmosphere determined to destroy its power.

Fear is determined to steal our joy, break our will, kill our faith, make a problem bigger than it is, cripple our decision making and make sure that life is lived under a ceiling which limits most possibilities. Fear is one of the world's biggest evil powers that can render the seemingly invincible to become powerless and pathetic. Fear creeps into our souls and steals our confidence. It whispers lies and twists facts. Fear needs to be conquered. The ceiling that fear can put over our lives needs to be smashed. We need to feel angry that fear has held us back and caused us to retreat into living with dysfunction and pain as if it were normal. The power of fear needs to be uncovered and broken over our lives.

As usual, we are often unaware of the fear that has a hold on us because our professional self seems to face little fear. This is because our vulnerable self has made decisions which try and protect us from feeling fear. It's easy to avoid close relationships, risks to our comfort, dangerous assignments, financial risks or any other situation where we don't feel empowered and in control. We need to be people who face our fears and see where we are held back or behaving in a dysfunctional way so that we can overcome.

Many people are aware of their struggle with fear. They are extremely conscious of living with a fear of accidents, illness, death or disaster. Many others live with a fear of terrorists, rapists, bombs, or gangs. Others struggle with a fear of the unknown, being powerless, being victimized, or being made redundant. Still others would laugh at these fears but actually have a deep rooted problem with the fear of failure, fear of rejection or fear of abandonment. There are so many areas where we can subconsciously allow fear to be the dominating emotion which can rule our decisions, small or large. Fear can lead us to stay with the same issues, shop in certain places, travel on certain roads, find employment at certain places and eat certain foods. We can live our lives trying to avoid having to face fear.

It is also an emotion which shows that we are alive and we want to stay alive, which is great. Fear can be a positive emotion which acts as a boundary to keep us safe, like the fear of electricity, or poisonous snakes. Often we are aware of fear but with reasoning and experience, 'feel the fear and do it anyway.'

For many people though, it is a crippling emotion where they are ruled, dominated and disabled by it. Jesus wants us to live a confident life where, in the face of fear speaking loudly to our souls, we have the louder voice of God's truth resounding. He died that we may live a life of freedom from disabling fear. He wants us to live a life of confidence, peace, assurance and trust. Let's look at where fear has a hold on us, that we may see its hold broken today and forever!

The cloak of victory

As was mentioned earlier, there is a cloak of victory which we can all wear to build faith and defeat fear. This cloak is spoken of in the Bible when soldiers came back from battle, their torn garments covered in stains of blood and mud. We too, have 'garments' which are covered with memories of battles we have seen won, and experiences where we have seen victories happen. Think back to times where you have seen miracles, answers to prayers, and other times where you have chosen and fought to overcome, rather than live under the power of fear or self pity. These memories are testimonies to God's power and faithfulness in the details of our lives.

In the Old Testament the leaders would often pray in times of challenge by first dwelling and focusing on all the major miracles and times of overcoming that they had experienced or their forefathers had told them about. They would then thank God for those times where victory had taken place and this in itself would enable them to see their present difficulties in context to these times of conquest.

This is a principle that we use a lot without necessarily noticing. I have just sat on a plane travelling to Prague questioning why we all have such extraordinary faith in aeroplanes! I have no idea at all how a plane flies despite many people having tried to explain it to me. My brain switches to 'bored mode' and something inside me seems to shut down as soon as these helpful souls try and teach me these basics of aerodynamics. I guess the reason so many of us unscientific types have such confidence in flying is the testimonies of all the people who have flown successfully for years. People who are afraid of flying teach themselves that there is no need to be afraid by reminding themselves of all the facts and statistics of the years of successful journeys where there have been no disasters or tragedies.

Choosing to 'put on the cloak of victory' by remembering those times of victory and being thankful for them is a powerful weapon of faith which breaks the power of fear in our daily lives. We are told frequently in the Bible to 'be thankful in all circumstances' and this is key because it changes our perspective and thinking about the future. It raises faith.

A possible definition of fear could be 'a strong belief in the possibility of disaster and negative outcome'. Another definition of faith could be 'the strong belief in the possibility of God's power changing a situation to bring a surprising and positive conclusion.' Where should we invest our strong belief?

The cloak of victory which can be used to defeat fear, I picture as being covered in photos of victories achieved. For example, reminders of the times where we battled in prayer over an illness and became healed, the times where we saw a financial miracle or maybe where we were able to be used as a vehicle to see someone else's life changed. Maybe the victory was achieved because we walked through difficult times and kept an attitude of faith and overcoming rather than self pity and grumbling. Maybe the fact that we made it through the hard times is victory in itself. The victory could be where we overcame an addiction or rose above temptation to be selfish or vindictive? Whatever victories we have won, we now have these experiences as a part of who we are. They are testimonies of success! In the book of Revelation, it is written that there is power in these stories which can change our present world as we remember them.

'And they overcame him because of the blood of the lamb and because of the word of their testimony'   *Revelation 12:11*

As we become thankful for the times where we have seen victory, we can face our present and future with a different attitude. We are taught in the Bible that we are *'transformed by the renewing of our minds'* (Romans 12:2). One thing that we can do immediately is to actively put into our thinking the stories of victories that we have seen take place in our lives and the lives of the people around us. They don't even have to be our own stories and victories. We can meditate on other people's breakthroughs which can build our faith and break the power of fear. This cloak of victory, covered with great stories from our own lives, others lives and Bible characters lives can become a powerful weapon against fear and anxiety!

Perfect love casts out fear

In 1 John 4:18 it says, *'perfect love casts out fear'*. The original Greek here actually describes the perfect love of God 'throwing out fear'. There is no room for fear when God's love, and the revelation of it, fills the spaces in our hearts and minds. When we 'hide' in the presence of God and focus on Him and His love and power, fear cannot remain. One touch from the presence of God and fear is evicted. Learn to see the power of God evicting fear in your life.

When we live in the atmosphere of the presence of God, fear loses its grip as the true reality of the power and compassion of God becomes a norm for us.

We need to meditate on the method of 'betach.' (This is spoken of in more depth in chapter 2)

- Visualize the goodness and mercy of God following you all the days of your life.
- Picture the armies and the presence of God going before you to prepare your way.
- Picture the shield of God protecting you from onslaught.
- Picture the arms of God holding you from below as He carries you in His arms.
- Visualize the presence of God surrounding you completely.
- Picture angels encamping around you to bring deliverance.
- Visualize the tower of refuge, the shelter of the Most High and the shelter of His wings covering you completely

so that you can remain confident, bold and peaceful at all times.

If we draw near to God, we are surrounded by His presence which protects, comforts, brings rest and peace as we walk through all the ups and the downs of life. We have to practise 'dwelling' on this truth so that the power of fear is weakened and lost. We are transformed by the 'renewing of our minds' and one significant practise which sees our lives change is to practise focusing or dwelling on God.

To dwell is described in the Miriam-Websters Online Dictionary as 'to sit down, to remain, to settle, to abide, to establish, to continue, to return, to lurk, to endure, to inhabit, to marry, to bring again to, to tarry and to take'. So as we dwell, sit down, tarry, remain and settle in the presence of God, we can find rest in the shadow of the Almighty. To be in someone's shadow implies a close proximity to them. We need to spend time seeking intimacy with God, our Father. To know rest and protection we can't speak to God from a polite distance where we fear rejection or where we feel ashamed or afraid. We need to be free to walk boldly to the throne of grace, knowing that we are covered in a garment of salvation, made right by Jesus and free from the effects of sin and shame. We are adopted, loved and cherished by our father who longs for our presence.

The fear of disaster

We live with the media often asserting that we have to be careful and that we should teach our children to be prepared for any disaster that is awaiting us. The newspapers report continually on daily disasters which ensure that many people are living in tension waiting for the next nearest tragedy which 'could have been us.' However, we don't need to be worried and live in this fear when we have God in our world. We live with the creator of the universe surrounding us. The One who knows all things is walking with us.

Here is some of Psalm 91. Read it and ask God to help you really believe it.

'He who dwells in the shelter of the Most High will abide in the shadow of the Almighty.
I will say to the Lord, 'My refuge and my fortress, My God in whom I trust!'
For it is He who delivers you from the snare of the trapper and from the deadly pestilence.
He will cover you with His pinions, and under His wings you may seek refuge;
His faithfulness is a shield and bulwark.
You will not be afraid of the terror by night, or of the arrow that flies by day; of the pestilence that stalks in darkness, or of the destruction that lays waste at noon.
A thousand may fall at your side and ten thousand at your right hand, but it shall not approach you.'

Here are some other verses from the Bible which speak of our protection when we are choosing to walk closely to God. All the verses which describe this protection from God speak of 'dwelling in His shadow' and to be in someone's shadow implies living in close proximity to them. This tells us that the safest place on earth is to be in a relationship with God where He can walk with us, guide us and speak to us as we go through life. Anything which tries to stop us from total intimacy with God needs to be sorted out as this intimacy leads to protection.

'I fear no evil, for you are with me'   Ps 23:4

'The Lord is my light and my salvation; whom shall I fear? The Lord is the defence of my life; so whom shall I dread? When evil doers came upon me to devour my flesh, my adversaries and my enemies, they stumble and fell. Though a host encamp against m, my heart will not fear; though war arise against me, in spite of this I shall be confident.'   Psalm 27:1-3

To be free from a fear of disaster is to know peace in all circumstances. We are promised that the Holy Spirit will be given to us as a Counsellor and as the Prince of Peace. We are told that we can know His peace which passes all understanding as we stay close to Him and keep our eyes fixed on Him and not the situations which change around us.

The fear of failure or the false guilt of not being perfect

Many people struggle with a fear of failure! Ultimately a fear of failure is intrinsically linked with a fear of rejection. Being rejected is usually the only and most dreaded consequence of failure. It can be a very limiting factor in our life journey if we are afraid of failure. Failure seems to be decided according to the expectations that are held by us or others. People can be crippled by a fear of failure in relationships and yet be free to fail comfortably in their workplace. Others can be crippled by a fear of failure in their job and yet be quite content with failure in their hobbies or leisure activities. Some people live with a fear of any kind of failure because it causes them to feel worthless and devalued.

For many of us we were raised in an environment where we felt constant guilt for not being all that we were meant to be or for not totally fulfilling our parents hopes and dreams for us. This guilt can be a consequence of our perceived failure. This same guilt can often cripple us for the duration of our lives as we strive to be perfect, to be high achievers or to at least not fail in the things that we decide to do. Failure can cause us to reject and despise ourselves as we feel guilt and pain over not being all that we feel we were meant to be. For people who have no deep fear of failure, the acts of failing are not linked to their identity and self esteem. For people who struggle with a fear of failure, each and every

106

moment of failure begs the question of their value and worth and can even question the purpose of their existence.

For some people they have grown up in an atmosphere which they could control. If a child was adored too much or could change the family atmosphere to ensure happiness or peace, or parented their parents by counselling them, then that child as an adult can still feel the weight of others reactions, emotions and general happiness. This weight and responsibility can lead to a high level of stress which is experienced as fear of failing others or guilt for not ever quite being able to keep people happy all the time.

There are hundreds and thousands of extremely stressed high achievers who are actually driven by a fear of failure and a crippling sense of guilt whenever any slight failure is experienced which only leads to a higher degree of striving to avoid further failure. Whilst these people can be great employees as they work so hard and fruitfully, they are not people who know the freedom of living life in all its fullness! They are handicapped by a desire to be perfect, a desire to be totally accepted and a desire to be free from vulnerability and weakness which could lead to failure. Their failure could lead to rejection and this could lead to further self hatred and misery!

I have been married for about 13 years and in this time I have realised that I have spent a great deal of time trying to get my husband to feel intense guilt every time he failed! I have always had a hatred of failure and love the travel mug I once bought at Houston, USA airport which states, 'failure is not an option.' I have loved this mug and although have taught on the fear of rejection for years, have never realised that my own life was crippled by an intense hatred of failure which led to me working long hours and not finding relaxation a natural experience! I didn't seem to fear failure because I made sure that I only worked in areas where I was confident and could guarantee success! Every time my husband failed, I was shocked and laboured my point of how he must not do that again because his failure had implications on my life. I can honestly say that I have never succeeded in making him feel guilty and I have been led to be deeply frustrated and confused by his understanding of his futility and weakness. He has been quite happy to acknowledge his failures and sort them out without living under guilt or condemnation. I am now allowing God to help me grasp this truth as I endeavour to walk into areas where I will probably not achieve all that I want to! I still hate failure but I am learning to embrace the fact that it does happen and God's love for me doesn't change. In fact the world doesn't fall apart and I can just rely on God more and know His love, tenderness, restoration, forgiveness and freedom.

Healing can happen

God wants us all to know that He loves us and finds pleasure in us even though we are not perfect. He knows that we are vulnerable and needy people who need to be dependant on Him. We need God to help us to live a life which is abundant, free and overflowing! As we allow God to show us how He views our weakness and vulnerability as normal and not disastrous, we can lower the expectations we have of ourselves and enjoy His salvation and restoration of us and our failings. He is the one who can help us to fail less, but also to deal with failure appropriately.

Jesus Himself was seen as a failure by many people during His earthly life. He was born in dubious circumstances, which would have led to immediate rejection from some. Then, once he begun to teach, preach and see healings there were many people who told Him that He was failing the Jewish laws and failing their expectations. He was constantly surrounded by an atmosphere of failure but He did not come under guilt or feelings of failure because He knew what He was called to do and knew that many would not approve.

We need to know the truth so that the truth will set us free. Once we know our illogical strongholds, we are in a position to fight to see truth take hold. We can allow God to heal our hearts from the pains of failure, the shame of our vulnerability and humanity and see ourselves as God sees us. We can experience

God's love as we sit in His presence and find healing and restoration and truth.

Fear not, stand still and see the victory which the Lord will give.   *Exodus 13:14*

The fear of rejection

The fear of rejection is one of the biggest disabilities which people struggle with in our society. It is hard to live life without being rejected or being disapproved of in some way. For many people they have lived their whole lives in an atmosphere of rejection. God wants us to know freedom from the fear of rejection. No-one likes to be rejected and it's never great to be disapproved of or to be misunderstood or unloved, but we need to know if we are actually living life with a real stronghold of a fear of rejection.

The atmosphere of rejection can be very painful even when there are no actual words or actions of rejection. We can sense and pick up on atmospheres where we are not understood and this can sometimes hurt far more and cause confusion as we work out why we feel pain.

I was talking to a teacher friend who had been tutoring a small group of children. She was telling me about one child who had left the group. Although nothing negative had been said to her by the others, she had noticed that they had all been subtly unwelcoming. The child had therefore been sitting in an atmosphere of rejection where she had struggled to feel accepted and justifiably wanted to get out of it! This teacher commented on the power of atmosphere and how hard it was to change this culture into a more loving environment.

The fear of rejection leads to so many ceilings on our life. The consequences can be that we avoid real intimacy, avoid relationships and don't experience freedom to enjoy the life which God wants us to live.

If we struggle with a fear of rejection we need to spend a little bit of time asking God where it first settled in us. Then we can take these memories to Jesus and ask that the healing power of Jesus brings freedom from pain and hurt in the memories. The power to set people free from the fear of rejection is found in grasping the unconditional love of Jesus. As our hearts grasp the reality of God's unfailing and extensive love, vast as the oceans; our hearts begin to care less and less what others think of us anyway. Healing and restoration penetrate our hearts as we bathe in His acceptance.

Irrational fear

Some people struggle with what seems to be irrational fear, but all fear has a reason somewhere! Most fear is usually rooted somehow in a fear of rejection, powerlessness, failure or abandonment. If you suffer from panic attacks or strange bouts of anxiety then ask God where it comes from. Ask yourself when you first felt that feeling of fear and then invite Jesus to speak truth about it into your heart.

God can break the power of every fear and set you free, no matter how big the fear. All things are possible with God, no matter what diagnosis you have had or how many generations have struggled in the same way. Don't allow your heart to settle for less than total freedom! Spot fear and see God pull the roots out and set you free from it!

Be strong and courageous, for you shall go with this people into the land which the Lord has sworn to their fathers to give them, and you shall give it to them as an inheritance. The Lord is the one who goes ahead of you; He will be with you. He will not fail you or forsake you. Do not fear or be dismayed.'
                                   Deut 31:7-8

Fear of God

There are many people that have spoken about being afraid of God. They express their anxieties about His power, judgement, holiness and might. The Bible talks about the benefits of 'fearing God' but this is actually recommending that we meditate and dwell on God's power and strength as an extraordinary fact, coupled with his mercy, compassion, love and tenderness. The word 'fear' in this context does not in any way mean that we are to be frightened or terrified of God. In fact as we dwell on God's holiness and power and develop a reverent awe of God as well as a passion and love for Him, this will enable and create an atmosphere in our world where fear can have little hold! The actual fear of God can break the power of unhealthy fear! An appropriate fear of God breeds peace and safety. Peace replaces anxiety and panic. Peace is such a dominant manifestation of the presence of God that one of the names of God is 'Prince of Peace.'(Isaiah 9)

In the Bible in the book of John (chapter 14:27) we read,

'Peace I leave with you, peace I give to you, not as the world gives do I give to you. Do not let your heart be troubled, nor let it be fearful.'

The power of the presence of God brings peace, liberty and joy as we learn to trust Him with all of our lives. The power of fear can be completely broken as we learn to see the power of God throw away the power of fear! It breaks the chains that bind us as we let Him take precedence in our lives. Teach yourself the truth of who God is because the enemy wants to keep you away from intimacy with Him, as he knows that being close to God brings freedom and boldness.

Practical steps to breaking the power of fear in our lives

Sometimes we can see the power of fear broken in our world when we put ourselves practically into a situation which stretches us and causes us to rely on God. Often as we make decisions to break into new areas of challenge, fear can arise. This could be applying for a new job, inviting someone new around for a meal, taking up a new position, trying something new for the first time or anything else which is not comfortable for you. This can be a great opportunity to press into God and be victorious. The victory comes when the fear that we feel is replaced by peace which in turn develops into confidence.

As God heals your heart, memories can resurface from long ago. These can often hold keys to our present reactions and emotional hurts. God wants to heal these and bring release from the pain that they carry. As we spend time in the presence of Jesus, these memories will often become naturally less full of negative emotions until there is clarity and peace. For people who have lots of painful memories, I use the illustration of balloons to explain why I believe it is worth pursuing the healing of them. I see that in all of us we carry red and black balloons which fill our internal worlds. Any negative, traumatic memories are like black, heavy, depressing balloons that cause pain and irritation. These black balloons are filled with dirt and weigh heavily in our souls and drain our energy and zeal for life whilst the red ones are reminders of happy, special times. Each time we see God heal a memory, another black balloon is popped, de-powered and the heavy contents drain away. Often there are many balloons attached to each other, so when one is popped, many others are de-powered too. So keep going! Pop those memories and see your life become empowered with God's perspective and truth. Make more room for the red balloons full of joy, testimonies and overcoming!

Fear is a reality for all of creation but God gives us the answer to living life as an overcomer where fear doesn't have a hold on our lives. We must actively renew our minds by dwelling on God, His nature, His miracles, His promises and all that He has done in our lives. As we do this, the power of fear will be weakened and will be conquered.

If you want to see the power of fear broken in your life you could pray something like this:

Father God,
Thank you that you know me and know where fear has taken me captive and disabled me from being all that you want me to be. God, I ask that you will help me as I determine to renew my mind by meditating on you, your power and your faithfulness. I want to see faith built into my heart with expectation as I trust you. I ask that you will show me where fear has come into my life so that I can see the roots dug.

Thank you that with you I am an Overcomer and nothing is impossible for those who believe.
Amen

Chapter 7

Back to basics- the needs of a child

'Mummy! Mummy! Mummy! Where are you?'

I can hear the sounds of doors slamming and the repetitive shouts of my name!

'Oh here you are, mummy.'

'Yes, hi there darling, are you alright? What do you want?'

'Oh nothing, I just wanted to find you that's all. I love you!'

'I love you too, very much! Do you want a cuddle?'

'nah thanks, later!'

And with that, the little feet scamper happily off to play earnestly again. It doesn't happen that often in our house but it happens often enough to remind me of my overall role in the home. Our home is such that there are one or two rooms which lie out of the general shouting range of the children. This is useful when my eldest son is practising the drums so he can play loudly and passionately and we are able to continue with all our activities undisturbed. (After all, why would you play the drums quietly? What would be the point?!) However, occasionally it does mean that the children can 'lose' me for a little while and go on a search to 'find me' usually because they didn't listen when I announced my intended plans to check my emails in the study, for example. The children want to know where I am because it reassures them and provides them with a sense of security and comfort.

We need to look at the most foundational stage of our lives, in order to see our hearts or vulnerable selves becoming restored and healed, so that they can become the conception place of success. We need to look at what has had the most profound influence in who we are now. Our childhood family homes are the place of huge significance in moulding us to become who we are today. Even if we have tried to deny the power of our early experiences in the forming of our identity, it becomes apparent that both the negative and the positive experiences of childhood are influential. Memories of many childhood events can give us keys into where some internal decisions were made and where wounds and negative emotions were felt or buried. In the process of trying to lose much of the excess emotional weight that we carry with us, we need to look at these early moments and allow our hearts to be honest about what needs and longings were or were not met. In this place of honesty, we can allow God to heal our hearts and bring transformation to our present.

The ideal family atmosphere

The word 'family' is becoming increasingly difficult to understand. It is a concept which has different connotations for everybody. We can often have a picture of what we believe to be an ideal family in our imaginations and many of us who are parents expend a great deal of energy and time trying to fulfil these hopes and dreams. What is a healthy family and what does it really look like?

I believe that the atmosphere which is most consistent in the family home is a clearer indication of family health rather than any other factors. Atmospheres can't be faked. They are what they are! The irony is that if we are too stressed trying to create the perfect family atmosphere, then the dominant atmosphere in our homes could possibly be stress, tension and anxiety despite the outward appearance! The atmospheres contain the events in them. Traumatic circumstances that happen in a home cause a change in atmosphere. Violence in the home is a harmful action in itself which also can produce an atmosphere of anger, fear, anxiety and panic. You don't have to be on the receiving end of the violent act to be affected adversely by the atmosphere it creates.

The atmosphere which speaks of the ideal family is the atmosphere of love. This is the intended atmosphere of family life which God designed for us as a greenhouse to nurture young, tender life. It is best described in the Bible in 1 Corinthians 13:

'Love never gives up. Love never cares for others more than self. Love doesn't want what it doesn't have. Love doesn't strut, doesn't have a swelled head, doesn't force itself on others, isn't always 'me first', doesn't fly off the handle, doesn't keep score of the sins of others, doesn't revel when others grovel, takes pleasure in the flowering of truth, puts up with anything, trusts God always, always looks for the best, never looks back, but keeps going to the end. Love never dies.'   *The Message Bible*

An atmosphere where real love is the dominant experience is an atmosphere where the needs of children are met, where they do not have to create internal emotional mechanisms to defend their vulnerability, needs and longings.

For many people, their childhood homes were not places filled with love and freedom due to the pressures that so many adults face with their own wounds and stresses. For many people they experienced atmospheres and events as children which have caused them to carry wounds and scars in their hearts which need to be admitted and healed. It's not about apportioning blame to anyone but merely taking responsibility ourselves for the effects that we now carry with us which could also damage the next generation. The purpose of this chapter is to look at the possible hurts and needs which are still present in our lives where we need to see God heal and restore us. He wants to bring His truth into our hearts to enable us to be all that we are meant to be. It's about enabling us to have true intimacy with God and know His love whilst enjoying relationships with others. Let's remove anything which hinders this!

The main role of a mother

Let's now look at the main role of a mother in a home and what the child needs to receive from her in their childhood. This helps us to see where we carry wounds which we need to ask God to heal. We must make sure that we don't allow self pity to rise inside of us. Self pity is a killer! It's a danger to our hearts because it actually stops healing take place. The perspective is simple; most of us haven't had ideal conditions to grow up in but God wants us to look at where we were hurt so that we can find healing and restoration in order to be more emotionally functional. As mothers reading this section, we must resist the temptation to become further entrapped in the guilt which so easily becomes the norm in this role. We must recognise that whilst we need to repent when God reveals any mistakes that we have made as mothers and we need to ask God for help and wisdom continually in parenting, ultimately we have to trust our children to God to restore any mess to become their message.

The mother is designed to be the primary **nurturer** of the children, where their needs are noticed and met. The child needs to be cherished and adored by their mother who signs herself up at birth as their biggest fan until they get married! When a child feels rejection for being the wrong gender, the wrong time or just wrong in some way, this can be highly damaging because to be adored is a core need. The child can experience the same level of rejection if they are the ones who are needed to bring the family hope or help. In these situations, it appears outwardly as though the children are adored or cherished, but actually they are being cherished for how they make their parents feel. This can be so subtle but extremely damaging. If a child is relied upon to be the atmosphere lifter or to heal a marriage for example, they will feel powerfully rejected in their subconscious because they themselves as people are being rejected. As they fulfil the role of helper they are being loved, but this can often be counterfeit love. This can be often phrased as 'we can't be at fault for loving you too much.' It's a love which meets the need of the parent and causes the same consequences as total rejection because the child is rejected as an individual person. Rejection can cause deep emotional pain which needs God to minister healing to.

A child also needs to have *affirmation* constantly from their mother. They should feel that they are great people to be around. Most people are valued for what they do and say, but real love affirms the value of the person as an individual. The child needs to feel that they have value for who they are, not just for what they are good at. This is communicated verbally and practically by quality time being spent together in a happy atmosphere where the mother and child enjoy each other's company. Many children are not encouraged because the parent can fear that they will become proud and arrogant or because they themselves were not encouraged as children. This can lead to an intense desire to experience affirmation from any person who is respected in the life of the adult. It can become an addictive cycle which can emotionally exhaust the adult as they spend time still looking for that feeling of being affirmed and encouraged.

The mother is designed to be the one who takes care of **the *details*** of a child's life. The small things are often the big things to a child. Wearing the right outfit, taking the right present, remembering the parties and homework jobs, washing the clothes in time for the next event, buying the right size clothes, remembering the playtime snack! As a mother cares for these details, it demonstrates her love practically. If a mother is physically absent or she just doesn't seem to manage to care for detail consistently for some reason, the child will often feel neglected. When a child feels this lack of love, they can often feel an intense guilt for being or doing something wrong. Subconsciously, children can often take the blame for any lack of love as a way of understanding their needs not being met. They can then carry this false guilt which can develop into shame in adulthood as an emotional burden.

The child also needs to experience *physical love* from their mother. Touch is powerful and experiments have been performed to see the consequence of a lack of touch in childhood. It has been proved that touch is healing, restoring and vital for life. A child needs to experience the comfort of being held and cuddled. Not a quick cuddle when a child has injured themselves but a clear and constant communication of love and affection. Often people in prayer times in church express that huge powerful desire to be held by a woman in a comforting, maternal manner because they still have a vacuum in their vulnerable self where they were not held frequently. If the atmosphere in the home was dominant with fear and anxiety, the cuddles could have been painful experiences which actually caused more fear rather than reassurance. If the mother was emotionally frozen, the cuddles would often be where the heart (and source of emotional love) was hidden and subsequently they could have felt more like a clinical experience than a fountain of love, nurture and acceptance.

The child also needs to enjoy time to *communicate* with their mother in a way where they can talk from their hearts about their real feelings, thoughts and worries. Many people who as adults find that they have got frozen emotions are in that place because they did not practise talking from their vulnerable self as children. Children need to talk about their daily experiences but they also need space and time to feel safe enough to tell their mum how they feel about the little things in their world. They also need to trust their mum that when they express these thoughts and feelings they won't be greeted with comments like, 'don't be ridiculous! How can you think that! Haven't you got more important things to think about?' Comments like this can devalue the child's thought life and can damage their trust in their mum's care for them. A child needs to feel understood and accepted as they are, without having to conform to what they believe they should think or feel.

The child also finds security seeing the mother acting as a *wife*. It helps the child to feel that there is a secure foundation of love in the family which will continue when the child becomes an adult and leaves the home. To see their mum and dad demonstrate love for each other is one of the most powerful ways of providing a feeling of security in a home. Where this love hasn't been modelled, the child can feel confused about their role and subsequently remain unsure about marriage or love as an adult. When unclear boundaries have been present and the child has been exposed to private bedroom scenes, this can also lead to fear and uncertainty as an adult.

As we have revelation of where we have been hurt by our mothers, we are not being disloyal, but acknowledging that they probably tried their best with what tools that they had. Very few mothers hurt their children on purpose, even the ones who seem to, don't really want to. Most are disabled emotionally by their own experiences and so they are actually expressing the wounds in their own hearts. This is not about apportioning blame but instead grasping where God needs to heal and restore us, in order for us to have whole hearts.

As part of dealing with the healing of our vulnerable self, we can see where we experienced less than God intended and allow him to heal us.

The role that fathers were intended to play

We are living in a fatherless generation where fewer and fewer children experience an active father living with them. The days of physically absent fathers is on the increase and many of the fathers who do remain living with their children and their mothers are often emotionally absent due to exhaustion from earning money. God is described as our heavenly father and Jesus explains beautifully how this role was intended to function. In Chapter 3, there are two powerful stories from the Bible which help us to understand God as our father who has adopted us as His children. We can picture the father who runs down the road with his arms out as the prodigal son returns home, tired and ashamed. The son is given a ring, the best robe and sandals to celebrate his return. Throughout the Bible, there are descriptions of God as a loving father who delights, cherishes and adores His children. If you are a single mum reading this section, please do not feel weighed down with guilt and note that God can be both husband and father.

The primary role of a father is one of *protection*. Where a mother protects her children with attention to detail and communication, a father protects with his strength. A dad should be there as a primary protector of his children. No matter what a child faces amongst his or her peers, there should be an innocence in their early years that totally believes that 'daddy can do anything' and 'my daddy is bigger and stronger than your daddy!' Even if their daddy is not huge and full of muscles, the child will still naturally look to him as a source of strength and protection. It is this strength which allows the child to feel secure as they grow up, knowing that someone would be there to defend them if they got hurt. Many people who have grown up without a father protecting or defending them feel exposed and wounded. This can be in the case of either physically absent or emotionally absent fathers. If the father is physically present but is not involved in the child's life due to tiredness, illness, emotional frozenness or passivity then the child can grow up with a feeling of isolation and abandonment. As an adult, they could still face that feeling of intense loneliness or fear of abandonment which God wants to meet and heal.

Part of the feeling of that protection comes from experiencing the **embrace of a father**. The strength which a child feels as they are held by their father is a comforting and affirming experience. Without the affirmation of touch, many people can feel lonely and isolated in their hearts no matter what their present experiences hold. Many people still subconsciously look for that same feeling of being held by their father as adults which can be confusing. God, our heavenly Father, can meet those needs that many face when they haven't had consistent hugs from their father

Another role of a father is one of **delighting in their children and affirming their gender**. A little girl needs her father to delight in her beauty by verbalising that affirmation and noticing her beauty. She longs to feel like the prettiest princess in the world and needs her father to affirm that. The little boy needs to be affirmed in his strength and 'manliness'. He longs to 'help his dad' with manly chores which require strength where he is proving to himself that he can be like his daddy. His dad needs to voice affirmation of his 'manliness' and invest his time to 'work together' on projects where this can be vocalised naturally. Children can be seriously wounded when the father doesn't affirm the child's gender or teases them about their beauty or strength. Many people live their whole life with parts of their body that they despise because they were teased or called a nickname which mocked that area. The power of these words needs to be broken and the area of the body which was cursed needs to be accepted. Words are powerful and when a core need is not met and instead the child receives mocking, they can become insecure and confused about their gender. Sadly, a child often doesn't experience this affirmation. Many men are still trying to prove their manliness often through sexual conquests and women are trying to be affirmed in their beauty often by being seductive. Obviously the most serious violation of a child's need for being delighted in is where a father misuses his boundaries and abuses his child. When a father speaks inappropriately by commenting on a child's beauty or manliness with a sexual overtone, this is confusing and harmful. The most severe damage to a child from a father is physical or sexual abuse. This can be extremely damaging to the child's understanding of love, gender and power and produces a great deal of fear in the adult survivor. God can heal the wounded heart and can put back the fragmented pieces of a person's heart where they have been so badly violated. Total healing can be found in Jesus!

The traditional understanding of the role of father is one of *provider*. When the Father provides financially for the children's needs, it can contribute to a family atmosphere full of peace and relaxation. These days, most families have several earners and this is not such a clear role to be taken. However, the children still feel protected and provided for when they have a father in the home which leads to that sense of safety and peace. Financial tension is the primary cause of unhappy atmospheres in homes. It's the primary cause of marital strife and divorce.

Finally, the children gain a sense of safety and comfort from seeing their father act in the role of **husband**. Again, it is inappropriate and harmful for them to see any sexual activity but it is extremely comforting for them to feel the atmosphere of love and affection which creates a beautiful nurturing atmosphere. For many people today God is the only source of comfort for the wounds of being fatherless. He can heal these wounds because he is the very Father which our hearts long for. As we allow Him to father us now, our past wounds can become healed and restored.

God is the only true father who can heal our hearts

God is the perfect Heavenly Father who demonstrates His love to His children as we learn to tune ourselves in to hear Him and spend time with Him. We need to realise that we will all view God from our vulnerable self as being like our earthy father, even when our minds comprehend the difference. It's a natural reaction from our hearts that were meant to experience an earthly father, who modelled Gods fathering nature. As we realize this, we can see that it is vital to spend time allowing God to show us what He is really like, in order to bring healing. Look at this description of His love towards us.

'The Lord your God is with you, he is mighty to save. He will take great delight in you, He will quiet you with his love, He will rejoice over you with singing'.
Zephaniah 3:17 N.I.V

The word 'rejoice' literally means 'to jump up and down and dance for joy'. That's what God does when He sees us. He is not passive or quiet in His love but actively demonstrates of His adoration for us, His children. How does that make you feel?

Hosea 11 beautifully explains the role of father that God had over the Israelite people in the Old Testament. The verse applies to us too as people who once ignored God but are who now actively seeking to follow Him.

'When Israel was only a child, I loved him. I called out, 'My son'- called him out of Egypt. But he ran off and left me. He worshiped the popular sex gods, he played at religion with toy gods. Still, I stuck with him, I led Ephraim. I rescued him from human bondage, but he never acknowledged my help, never admitted that I was the one pulling his wagon, that I lifted him like a baby, to my cheek, that I bent down to feed him....'   The Message Bible

That is not a description of an angry judge who is waiting to catch us in sin and punish us. This is a description of a Father God who is patient and merciful. He is described as longing for us to realise His love and enjoy it. God wants to reveal the extent of His love and strength to our hearts where we have been hurt and disappointed.

Jesus then talks like this about fathers:

'Or what man is there among you who, when his son asks for a loaf will give him a stone? Or if he asks for a fish, he will not give him a snake will he? If you then, being evil, know how to give good gifts to your children, how much more will your father who is in heaven give what is good to those who ask him'.
Matthew 7:9-10

So we have a father in heaven who wants to shower us with blessings! That's demonstrative love which can take our breath away!

The following verse describes the intimacy that we can have with God. So whilst we understand that He is mighty, powerful, and the creator of all things, we can also know real intimacy with him which heals these wounds from our childhood.

'Thus, we have now been set free to experience our rightful heritage. You can tell for sure that you are now fully adopted as his own children because God sent the spirit of his son into our lives crying 'Papa, father!' Doesn't that privilege of intimate conversation with God make it plain that you are not a slave, but a

child? And if you are a child, you're also an heir, with complete access to the inheritance.'
Galatians 4:6-7 The Message Bible

When Jesus taught his disciples how to pray, the name that he used was, 'Our Father.' This emphasises the importance of the nature of God as our father and maybe the 'daddy' that we never had? We need to understand God as our father in order to heal those wounds of unmet needs and longing which can weigh us down with sadness, emptiness, guilt and sorrow. Our heavenly father brings healing to the most broken hearted. Let's take some time to imagine ourselves running with confidence and boldness to our Daddy God where we are greeted with pleasure and delight! Let that begin to become a reality in our hearts.

If it helps, you could pray something like this:

Father God,
Thank you that you are my Father. Come and heal any wounds which lie in the depths of my soul where there are unmet needs and pains from my experiences as a child. Let me know you as the true father who can meet every need that I carry with me and heal every wound which I feel. Show me where I react in dysfunctional ways, that I may know total healing and wholeness. May I increase in my revelation of your love for me continually as I enjoy your presence.
Amen

James' Story

Slowly and surely the car pulled away, crunching the gravel and made its way up the extensive drive. The young lad aged six watched alone at the leaded window, 'Daddy's going, daddy's leaving', were the numbing words that echoed on his insides.

Some ten years later while praying in a small group, one of the guys spoke out, 'James I think there's something about your dad that God wants to deal with'. At that moment the memory of my dad driving out of the family home for the last time was brought back to my memory. I had come to know Jesus some 9 months before and had never realised my dad's leaving had effected me. With the memory came all the feelings of loss, rejection, abandonment and sorrow that I had suppressed in order to cope as a six year old. This time however, I was not alone but as the feelings came flooding back I was able to 'cry them out' and give them to Jesus. The pain was so overwhelming but having 'cried out' the loss the memories were no longer painful and the ache had gone.

This was the start of Jesus' restoration process in my life. I had never attributed that my lust for success and significance on the sport's field, my constant desire to please people (being good enough), my pursuit of physical gratification through pornography and relationships all stemmed from this loss and rejection in my early years.

Over the next few years God started to reveal how He felt towards me and how I needed to view myself through His eyes rather than my experiences to date. The path leading to healing is not pain free. Jesus however does guarantee that if we are willing to hand over our sorrows they can be placed on the cross. There have been times where I have been hesitant to make this exchange because of the fear of facing these wounds. It is at this point that I have learnt to push through and face the grief in order to give it to Jesus and to take His peace and wholeness. The pain when faced in this way is less than living with the ongoing pain and consequences of coping with the wounds. The challenge that I have faced on numerous occasions when God puts His finger on an area of my life is; do I care more about the opinions and thoughts of those around seeing me 'undergoing God's surgery' or do I care more about having the Creator and Healer touch my world restoring me to His image.

Georgina's Story

In my late thirties, I had an unprompted retrieval of memory of sexual abuse as a young child. The retrieval was of one incident but my sister who had been present (but never talked about it until I asked for verification of the incident) told me there had been others.

My first reaction was one of pain, emotionally and physically, quickly followed by shame. My husband, when I told him, was very supportive. We cried.

Amazingly, just a few months before, my husband had become a Christian and we started going to church. I had some counselling and prayer support at that time. Life carried on. I worked, carried on bringing up 3 children, got to know God better, but felt like a part of me still felt deeply sad, and I cried a lot.

At church the teaching begun to have a huge impact on me. One evening in a prayer meeting I felt prompted by God to ask for more prayer to be specifically centred on the abuse. One of our senior pastors asked me if I had forgiven myself. It was as though the lights went on. I had come to terms with the abuse and forgiven the abuser but I became aware that I had blamed myself. As I prayed, I felt the presence of God enwrap me and felt released from the power of false guilt and shame. The joy that bubbled up in me has never stopped and I can still recall the feeling of freedom and liberty.

The pain and shame I had felt for so long had gone and I knew that I had received some powerful emotional healing.

Section 3
The Message

Empowered with a message to change the world...

Chapter 8

The power of a new name.

As we determine to allow God to heal, restore and transform our mess into our message, an important key is to see ourselves as God sees us. After a short time of exploring our hearts dysfunctions, it becomes imperative to stop searching and start actively speaking the healing of our hearts into existence. This is called faith not denial! Just looking at our dysfunction and pain doesn't bring healing, but allowing God to minister His love and his revelation of truth to our deepest pains can totally transform us. In the last seven chapters we have looked at the issues of shame, longings, fear, insecurity, hurt, disappointment and pain and we can find ourselves accepting labels and names for ourselves. These names and labels can be detrimental to our lives and stop us moving into increased freedom, confidence, boldness and liberty.

Names are important to God

The Bible contains lists and lists of names which give us an insight into God's heart which beats for individuals. He is passionate about each unique person alive and knows their name, their longings, dreams, fears and thoughts. He loves and adores every person created, wanting them to draw close to Him and experience His love and tenderness towards them.

I have three children here on earth alive and noisy, and two in heaven and I can tell you that I will never forget any one of those boys because they are engraved onto my heart. I can't help but love them as they are a part of my life. I love to just think about them and remember funny little moments when they've said something cute. I find myself smiling or even laughing out loud when I remember some times we've had together! Only yesterday two of my sons had a birthday party in the garden to celebrate their tenth and eighth birthdays. Much to all of our surprise, Andrew, my husband and their father and a ten year old guest fell backwards into our pond as they bounced off the top of the bouncy castle! It was such a funny sight as these two stood there covered from head to foot in slime and weed! There was even a tadpole or two that tumbled out of their pockets! We all laughed and laughed together as we questioned how it happened. I loved looking at my sons faces as they giggled and laughed. God loves to think about us and remember funny times when we have laughed and enjoyed his world. The Bible tells us that we are a delight to God. He knows our name, knows our thoughts and knows how many hairs are on our head.

New Names

There is great significance in our names which can often be overlooked. I once visited a church where a woman introduced herself to me by reaching out to grab my hand with intensity in her face saying, 'Hi, I'm Broken.' Although this is an unusual greeting, it speaks clearly of the way that many people carry subconscious names in their heads of who they are. I've met lots of young guys who introduce themselves to me as Dave or Steve when they are actually calling themselves names in their heads like 'babe magnet' and 'awesome stallion'! Does this sound familiar? We all carry names in our hearts. Good ones, funny ones, negative ones or fantasy ones which all have the power to put ceilings on our lives and disable our future success. These names can cause conflict in our soul if we don't vigilantly filter them

In the book of Revelation it talks about how God wants to give us a new name.

'To him who overcomes to him I will give a white stone, some of the hidden manna and I will give him a white stone and a new name

written on the stone which no one knows but he who receives it.'   *Rev 2:17*

In these times, the judges would communicate their decisions about someone's innocence or guilt by presenting either a white or a black stone. A black stone would be a declaration of the belief that the person being tried was guilty and the white stone would be a declaration of the belief in their innocence. In this verse, God presents us with a white stone as a symbol of our position with God. We are being declared free from the consequence of our sin because of Jesus blood. The new name which is given with the white stone is a powerful symbol of a new future, with new hope, a new re-birthed identity, and a new freedom with new possibilities. All the negative associations with the old name can be washed away into the past and a new start can be made. Freedom is proclaimed with a new identity and a new name.

In Isaiah 62 we are told of how God wants to change our name far removed from any negative associations with our past, which can change our future. Our hearts need to grasp the truth of our new name.

'You will be called by a new name which the mouth of the Lord will designate. You will also be a crown of beauty in the hand of the Lord, and a royal diadem in the hand of your God. It will no longer be said of you, 'Forsaken' nor to your land will it any longer be said to you 'desolate', but you will be called My delight is

in her' and your land 'Married'.
Isaiah 62:2b-4

You will no longer be called desolate and forsaken. These names need to be stripped off us as our hearts grasp how loved we are by God. God wants to strip off us some names which our culture or people in authority have put on us. Names like divorced, uneducated, simple, worthless, abused, idiot, failure, working class, stupid and victim. There are loads of names which attach themselves to our vulnerable self and hold us back from being all that we are meant to be.

God wants us to strip names off ourselves which we hold in our subconscious. 'I don't take risks,' 'I'm always ill', 'I'm old', 'I'm a simple kind, 'Our family don't do great things, we just get by'. There are words, names and sentences which act as a ceiling over our lives if we don't reject them. Any sentence which uses the words 'always' and 'never' acts as a powerful block to believing the truth about who we are as God sees us.

The power of words

God created the world by his words. In Genesis 1 we read the story of how the world came into being as God spoke.

'And God said...and it was.'

We have been created in the image of God and therefore just as God's words were creative, so also are our words. In the story of creation we don't see God mixing potions or going through some creative technique or formula apart from the creation of Adam and Eve, he just spoke!

As God created the world by the words that he spoke, we too must create our world by the words that we speak.

We need to be careful what we call ourselves and what we speak over ourselves because words have power. We must decide to agree with God's views and not the devils views about who we are.

'The one who desires life, to love, to see good days must keep his tongue from evil and his lips from deceit'
1 Peter 3:10 and Ps 34:12-14

With our tongue we can either bless or curse ourselves and others. We have been given the authority and the power to speak the names which God speaks over us. We can agree with God about our identity rather than agreeing with the devil.

In the areas of our life where we don't feel fruitful and successful the devil wants us to name ourselves and agree that we're barren and a failure. He wants us to give up trying to be anything else. Yet God looks at us and sees what we can be and re-names us 'fruitful'. In areas of our life that seem to be broken and full of pain we can speak over ourselves, *'No longer will I be called desolate...'*

143

As we agree with God about who we are, we are speaking in faith about our identity. God loves faith.

'Faith...calls into being that which does not yet exist'   *Romans 4: 4*

'Faith is...the conviction of things not yet seen'   *Hebrews 11:1*

We can speak over ourselves the names that God has given us and believe that this is who we truly are. As we consistently confess truth with our mouths, our hearts will cultivate seeds of truth into strong trees of confidence, boldness and assurance.

Recently my husband became 40 years old which we celebrated with great joviality. Soon, however, it seemed to be a significant pinnacle in my life as I faced for the first time that I was only 5 years younger and I felt I had to begin to prepare myself! My ponderings became a mid- life crisis as I publicly and privately declared my age, my husbands age and my feelings about ageing! Over a period of several months I had noticed that in order to prepare myself for 'getting older', I had started to say, 'Well I guess I'm old'. This statement turned to, 'I'm old aren't I.?' Unaware after several months of declaring this over myself, I began to be aware of looking older! I had actually grown my first grey hairs and my hands had started to look old and wrinkly! I had assumed that this was because 'I was getting old' until I had a wake up call from God about the name that I was calling myself. Immediately I repented about speaking negatively and broke the power of those words and all that I had created in my world by a mistake. I declared that I was young and beautiful and paid my kids more pocket money if they told me this truth! They obliged for a while! I already feel younger and was at a conference in Africa this last week where some young people in their twenties thought I was 28. How good is that!

Right now why don't you agree with God and call yourself blessed.

We are no longer desolate but cherished
We are no longer in captivity but free.
We are no longer in poverty but in abundance.
We are no longer in barrenness but fruitful.
We are no longer broken but restored.

Call into being that which does not yet exist. You may not feel these things but the Bible tells us that they are our inheritance. Faith speaks things into being before you feel and see them with your physical eyes. God is in you if you have given him rule over your life and therefore you have all the blessings, power, fruitfulness, abundance, prosperity and health already in you!

'Your body is the temple of the Holy Spirit'
1 Corinthians 6:19

It's a bit similar to really wanting to eat a cake and having a table with all the ingredients for a cake on it right in front of you. It isn't that hard to measure and mix the ingredients and put them in the right atmosphere to see the cake mixture becoming a cake. In the atmosphere of faith, we too can see dreams and new identities becoming a reality. We have all we need in us, we just have to speak the words and wait in the atmosphere of faith for the transformation of our minds and hearts.

Jesus was called many names by different people but He didn't agree with them or defend himself. He just stated who he was by saying, 'I am...the gate, the resurrection and the life, the good shepherd etc.' We need to re-write our names so that when we reply to accusations, jokes, comments and statements about who we are, we can reply with, 'I am...blessed, chosen, prosperous, fruitful...'

When we are feeling defeated or brokenhearted, we can say with fire in our hearts, 'I feel defeated or broken but I am the head and not the tail, the victor and the one loved by God.'

People in the Bible who had their names changed

Let's look at some people in the Bible who changed their names. Hebrews 11 is a chapter which is a bit like a hall of fame for mighty people of faith. It lists many of the mighty men and women of faith in the Old Testament. One of the common themes that all these people share is that they all had to battle to shake off their natural names, overcome those negative consequences and speak into being new names from God. They all had some fairly tough 'U' turns to make!

Noah was the only man, with his family who followed God in his whole generation. He was the only one to live a holy life, who was prepared to go against the flow of all his peers and build an ark when there was no sight of rain. He was prepared to be totally different from all the people around him. Can you imagine the names that he must have been called? Can you imagine him going home after a long day working on the ark? He probably had to spend time with God hearing who God said he was and rejecting those mocking names which must have been spoken over him and his family. He would have had to meditate on God's love, faithfulness and promises of protection and blessings as he washed away the words idiot, dreamer, freak and such like words out of his system. He carried on the task that God gave him, he overcame in his mind and his actions changed the course of history.

Jacob is the next man listed in this hall of fame. He had an unfair start to his life as he was only just born as the second twin. He was so close to getting all the blessings that were given to the first born and yet missed. How frustrating for him. So he cheated his brother out of this birthright and then had to run away to preserve his life. That's not a great way to begin a successful life. However, he ends up having an encounter with an angel where he shouts his frustration.

'I will not leave without a blessing from you!'
Genesis 32:26

He refused to live an unblessed, unsuccessful, second rate life. He was determined to know blessing. God changed his name during this angel experience. The Bible records:

'Your name shall no longer be Jacob but Israel'   *Genesis 32:28*

Jacob means 'deceiver' and Israel means 'chosen'. That's a great name change to celebrate. He got that which he was determined to have. How much do you want to see your future changed?

The chapter in Hebrews continues with Joseph who was a favourite son persecuted by his brothers, sold into slavery, put into prison and yet overcomes all odds to become a powerful leader in a powerful nation.

Moses is another overcomer who should have been killed at birth but was put into a basket which floated down a river into a new life in the palace as an adopted son of Pharaoh. He had a very shaky start in life but overcame the confusions of his identity to become a very influential leader of the people of God.

Rahab is a woman listed in this hall of fame who was born into a nation which didn't fear God. She had a revelation about God and risked her life to help the Israelite people and becomes the only person to be free and alive in the captured city of Jericho. She overcame the names which naturally should have caused her to be cursed from birth.

There is power from heaven released when someone overcomes the name that the devil has used to harm the people of God. There is a fragrance released when new names permeate into someone's soul to release them from the chains that hold them back. Authority is born. Power is released. Lives are influenced.

Peter was an extraordinary character in the Bible who also had a name change. He was originally called Simon but at a poignant moment Jesus turns to him and says,

'I also say to you that you are Peter and on this rock I will build my church and the gates of hell will not prevail against it.'
Matthew 16:18

The name Peter means 'large rock' which implies that he will be significant in the foundations of the building of Gods house. It's not a long time later when Peter denies knowing Jesus. Can you imagine Peter wrestling with his new name and wanting to take on names of failure, worthless, traitor, shame, and self hatred? Yet Jesus meets him soon after this moment and calls him Peter with absolute confidence. Our new names aren't dependant on our performance and perfection but on us accepting His help in our weakness and desire to become like him. In being 'In Christ' we are blessed, prosperous, fruitful and powerful. Outside of Him we are not much but lost.

All of these heroes of the faith would have had to work hard at not living under names like rejected, abandoned, alien, freak, alone, unwanted, persecuted and unloved and listen instead to what God was saying about them.

What voice are we listening to today? Are we listening to the voices which call us hopeless, rejected, failure, mediocre, unsuccessful, fearful or a disaster? Or are we tuning our ears to hear God's still small voice which is powerful enough to change our whole lives. He says over us that we are special, unique, precious, beautiful, strong, able and chosen. He has planned a good future for us with plans to prosper us and not to harm us.

Today why don't you decide that you won't settle for a mediocre life where names hold you back from all that you could and should be? Choose to listen to God about who you are and become the best you that you can be!

Pray now that God would help you get the revelation of who you are. Listen to him as he whispers what your new name is. Break the power in the name of Jesus of any names which have held you back from being all that God created you to be! Why don't you pray now?

Chapter 9

Walking in Authority and Abundance

'How precious is your loving kindness, O God! And the children of men take refuge in the shadow of Your wings.

They drink their fill of the abundance of Your house; and You give them to drink of the river of Your delights.

For with You is the fountain of life; in your light we see light.'

Psalm 36:7-9

We are a people loved, known and planned for by God. As His children He has plans to prosper us and bring us into a life of victory, breakthrough and abundance.

We are royalty. Our Father in heaven is the king of kings and we are His adopted children. We are important people who have a unique calling and destiny to fulfil.

It's time for the people in the house of God to put on their robe of authority. For those of us who have given our lives to Jesus we are the carriers of the presence of God.

'You are the temple of the Holy Spirit'
1 Corinthians 6:19

We are the ambassadors of the kingdom of God, and we are adopted children of the King of Kings. When we walk into a room, authority, power and the presence of God walks into that room with us. We are atmosphere changers and have the power to totally shift the environment around us. We can put on the robe of authority and rather than submit to the fear or discouragement in a room, we can bring an atmosphere of hope, faith and love. There is power in us. There is prosperity in us. There is blessing, hope, joy and life in us. We know this because once we've turned our life over to his leadership, the Holy Spirit lives in us. The Holy Spirit is God and so all the power of heaven lives inside of us. We are the earthen vessels which hold the treasure of heaven. Can you begin to grasp the possibilities there are for your life? We are world changers. We need to put on that identity as members of the royal family, with all of our fathers resources available to us to see his kingdom extended. His kingdom is a culture of love, hope, peace, patience, goodness, fun, laughter, mercy, joy, longsuffering, power, and kindness. What an incredible kingdom culture to bring to people. We are the carriers of the culture of the kingdom because we are part of the kings chosen family. We can walk with a strong sense of confidence and boldness in who we are, no matter what anyone thinks about us. We can take off any negative names that people have called us and take off any garments of shame or fear and put on the robe of authority and walk through life with an inner confidence and assurance of God's love and acceptance.

If at the moment you are a person who doesn't feel confident and you don't feel like a person of authority then its time to start using your words to build your world. Start to call yourself confident, bold as a lion, a man or woman of authority and wisdom as you 'call into being that which does not yet exist.' A shift will happen as your spirit grasps the truth! Your professional self is teaching and telling your vulnerable self the truth. Just watch your vulnerable self rise up with revelation and boldness!

The robe of abundance

There are many promises for the people of God. The children of a royal family have many promises for their present lives and inheritances for their future. Jesus has already died and risen again so we can have our inheritance now. It's there for us but we need to fight to get a hold of it because the enemy wants to kill, steal and destroy us and so is actively determined to stop us from having our inheritance. Let's look at the promises for those of us who are walking with Jesus as our Lord.

'Now shall it be if you diligently obey the Lord your God, being careful to do all his commandments which I command you today, the Lord your God will set you high above the nations of the earth.

All these blessings will come upon you and overtake you if you obey the Lord your God.

Blessed shall you be in the city and blessed shall you be in the country.

Blessed shall be the offspring of your body and the produce of your ground and the offspring of your beasts, the increase of your herd and the young of your flock.

Blessed shall be your basket and your kneading bowl.

Blessed shall you be when you come in and blessed shall you be when you go out.

The Lord shall cause your enemies to who rise up against you to be defeated before you, they will come out against you one way and will flee before you seven ways.

The Lord will command the blessing upon you in your barns and in all that you put your hand to, and he will bless you in the land which the Lord your God gives you.

The Lord will make you abound in prosperity...The Lord will open for you his storehouse , the heavens , to give rain to your land in its season and to bless all the work of your hand, and you shall lend to many nations and you shall not borrow.

The Lord will make you the head and not the tail, and you only will be above and not underneath, if you listen to the commandments of the Lord your God, which I charge you today to observe them carefully.

Deut 28: 1-8, 11-13

The robe of authority and abundance is put on us when we begin to act as the head and not the tail. We are not manipulated and moved around by everyone and the circumstances and atmospheres around us but we are the head, the leaders and the atmosphere changers. As an adopted child of the King of Kings, we are expected to know blessing. Members of a royal household have all that they need and more because that is a manifestation of that kingdom. We too, as children of the King have all we need and more because there are infinite resources in God's kingdom. You may not feel blessed or prosperous as you read this but you can start to speak words to create your world. Begin to take a hold of the inheritance that God wants to give to you by renewing and expanding your mind with truth.

'All these blessings will come upon you and OVERTAKE you if you obey the Lord your God'   *Deuteronomy 28: 2*

155

We can read here that God wants to give us blessing wherever we live. He wants to bless our children, our businesses, our homes and our travelling. He wants us to know abundance in our world that we might be a blessing to the nations. It's our job to bless the people in the world as we share the resources of heaven.

In the Bible there are so many promises about the provision of God. He is our heavenly Father who delights to give to us. As a mum, I totally adore giving presents to my children! It's such fun to shop for them knowing that what I'm buying will surprise and excite them. I love it on their birthdays when they run into our room expectant of the pile of presents that they will find wrapped for them. At the moment my littlest son just loves the experience of receiving gifts and is not particularly interested in the actual presents! He loves the experience of being the centre of attention as he is overwhelmed by our expressions of adoration. Our father in heaven 'delights in the prosperity of his people.' (Psalm 35:27) He wants us to enjoy his presents too.

In the book of Philippians 4:19 it says,

'My God will supply all my needs according to his riches in glory'

My children know this verse and stop me from ever confessing with my mouth that we can't afford anything. Everything is possible! Everything belongs to God! Often we have to be patient and keep believing when things don't look blessed. It's a fight of faith and the Bible tells us that any of us who live lives of faith are pleasing God.

'Without faith it's impossible to please Him'
Hebrews 11:6

Faith doesn't get developed overnight. It's a substance in your spirit which grows stronger as you choose to stand on the promises of God above everything else.

'...those who through faith and patience inherit the promises.'   *Hebrews 6:12*

We have to remember that every blessing comes from God and be thankful for everything that he showers on us.

'Every good and perfect gift comes from God'
James 1:17

Confidence in God

So we are a chosen people who can walk wearing a robe of abundance and authority. We can know peace and confidence as we learn to trust more and more in our heavenly Father. A man in the Bible called Job said some wise words about trusting God and not the abundance that comes from knowing God.
'If I have put my confidence in gold and called fine gold my trust, if I have gloated because my wealth was great and because my hand had secured so much...that too would have been an

157

iniquity calling for judgment, for I would have denied God above. *Job 31:24*

Confidence is something that many people would pay a high price for, but although clothes, position and popularity can help breed a degree of confidence, ultimately it comes from inside a person's soul. Many, many people are lacking confidence because they are trying to put their trust in the wrong things. In the book of Jeremiah in the Bible it says:

'Cursed is the man who trusts in mankind and makes flesh his strength and whose heart turns away from the LORD for he will be like a bush in the desert and will not see when prosperity comes but will live in stony wastes in the wilderness a land of salt without inhabitants. Blessed is the man who trusts in the LORD, for he will be like a tree planted by the water, that extends its roots by a stream and will not fear when heat comes. But its leaves will be green and it will not be anxious in a year of drought nor cease to yield fruit'. *Jeremiah 17:5-8*

We can put all our confidence and trust in the God who knows us so well. Our heavenly Father knows our thoughts, dreams, hopes and fears. It says that He knows how many hairs are on our head. He knows all about us. David says;

'He is intimately acquainted with all our ways, even before there is a word on our tongue, behold O LORD, You know it all'.
Psalm 139: 3

As we place our lives into His hands, we can trust that God knows even when we don't know. God loves and cherishes us even when we don't feel special. He is always with us even if we feel lonely. God has the power to change situations and when things go wrong we can know that He is with us and will protect us.

Trust in the LORD with all your heart and lean not on your own understanding. With all your heart ask Him and He will make your paths straight'. Proverbs 3:5

Our confidence needs to be found in God, not in our own intelligence and reasoning, but in His ways and timings.

The robe of authority

We are also called to actively bring the kingdom of God into the places where the enemy has taken rule. We live in a world where sickness, depression, poverty and devastation are a normal part of society. We are called to change this. We have the keys to set people free form sickness, poverty, oppression, depression, and devastation. There are no 'professionals' about to do this task. Don't look around your shoulder for someone else to do it instead of you! We are all called to change the world that we are in by bringing the kingdom of God into reign. Where there is a person who is sick, we are to pray for them to see them set free. Where there is someone who is depressed and brokenhearted, we have the keys of hope, healing and life to bring to them. We are able to walk with authority as people who hold keys to change lives. We hold the resources of heaven in us and are able to see lives be totally transformed.

When Jesus was talking to his disciples he said:

'Truly, truly, I say to you, he who believes in me, the works that I do, he will do also; and greater works than these he will do, because I go to the father. Whatever you ask in my name, that will I do, so that the Father may be glorified in the Son. If you ask anything in my name, I will do it.'

John 14:12-14

We don't walk in our own authority, but in the authority of Jesus who has called us and equipped us. We can be confident and bold in knowing that we are called to do extraordinary things in the name of Jesus. In our name, not much can happen, but when we do things in the name of the one who sent us, power is released. The world needs us to put on this robe of authority to see our own lives changed and to see others impacted and transformed with the presence of God. If we have feelings of insecurity and brokenness, we don't have to accept that that is how we'll always be. We can put on our robe of authority and walk with confidence in who we are, empowered to do the works of Jesus.

Sometimes I have prayed for people to get well and nothing has happened, but I won't let discouragement take root in me. I have also prayed for people and seen miracles happen where people are healed of enormous illnesses. I don't have to worry and be anxious about the results. I just need to be a person who has compassion on the people who God made and so desire to bring them into the freedom that God wants for them.

We have a commission on our lives where we need to walk in abundance so we can be a blessing and where we walk in authority so we can see lives changes and refuse to accept limitations. What an exciting life!

For I am planting seeds of peace and prosperity among you. The grapevines will be heavy with fruit. The earth will produce its crops and the sky will release the dew. Once more, I will make the remnant in Judah and Israel the heirs of these blessings. Among the nations, Judah and Israel had become symbols of what it means to be cursed. But no longer! Now I will rescue you and make you both a symbol and a source of blessing! So don't be afraid or discouraged but instead get on with building the temple.

In those days ten people from nations and languages from all around the world will clutch at the hem of one Jew's robe and they will say, 'Please let us walk with you for we have heard that God is with you!'

Zech 8:12-13, 23 New Living Translation

Why don't you pray right now that God helps you grasp your identity as one who walks as royalty with authority. Start today to renew your mind with the truth of the commission we have to be atmosphere changers and presence carriers. Allow your heart to expand with the understanding of who you have been called to be. See negative self images smashed as you grasp how God sees you!

Chapter 10

Tools for breakthrough

'But in all these things we overwhelmingly conquer through him who loved us. For I am convinced that neither death nor life, nor angels, nor principalities, nor any things present, nor things to come, nor powers, nor height or depth, nor any other created thing will be able to separate us from the love of God, which is in Christ Jesus our Lord'
Romans 8:37-39

'With God all things are possible'
Matthew 19:26

We are people who are designed to conceive and give birth to big dreams. God has put dreams into our hearts which will change the world and he longs to see them realized. He has given us everything we need to see these things come to pass and he wants us to experience His encouragement and His pleasure as we desire breakthrough. Sometimes, deep in our vulnerable selves we have bought the lie that God doesn't really want us to succeed and that He is sitting in heaven with his arms crossed, expecting us to fail. This is a lie! All of heaven is cheering us on to live a life full of success, overcoming and victory as we take territory, move obstacles out of our way and see the enemy defeated and Jesus kingdom extended.

The purpose of this book is to help people grasp all that God has for them so that we can see dynamic, effective carriers of the presence of God bringing the message of Jesus into this hurting world. We need to deal with our own issues if we are going to be effective at helping others. Throughout this book the danger of self pity or naval gazing has been emphasised as the worst consequence of looking at the depths of our hearts. We encourage people to have an overcoming approach to seeing their hearts become whole. A key to keeping a healthy attitude whilst God brings revelation to us is to keep God first in everything. Ultimately we want to remain God centred. If we become 'I' centred we lose all Godly perspective and will become increasingly dysfunctional, unbalanced and miserable. We need to put God first, and serve others whilst allowing time for ourselves to enjoy the healing power and presence of God.

There are some power tools which God has given to us to help defeat the enemy who seeks to wear us down. These tools will enable us to walk into victory and keep our hearts in a place which will facilitate our mess becoming a more influential message.

The first and greatest tool is that of prayer.

In James 5:16 it says, *'The prayers of a righteous person are powerful and effective.'*

The power of prayer as a tool to change lives is extraordinary. Prayer is simply talking to God and spending time in His presence. There is no religious formula for prayer but there are some suggestions from Jesus about how to pray most effectively. As we spend time communicating with 'Our Father' by telling him all about our thoughts, feelings, hopes, desires, hurts and disappointments we get healed. As we involve God in these things by talking to Him, we draw near to Him with all our hearts. It says in the Bible that as we *'draw near to God, he will draw near to us'. (James 4:8)* Prayer enables us to be intimate and close to our heavenly Father, the maker of all things. How awesome is that? As we spend time drawing near to God, we are able to listen to Him and hear revelations from heaven which can shift things in our world quickly and powerfully. Hearing wisdom, revelation and guidance direct from the Almighty God into our hearts is incredible! That's why so many of the writers and prophets of the Bible urge us to seek God with all our hearts.

Situations and strongholds which can take years to change can be shifted quickly when God speaks directly to our hearts. Seek God by waiting in his presence and having a heart which is teachable, hungry and reliant on his whispers. Develop a restless, eager, desperate desire to pursue God and please him in everything.

Remembering God's faithfulness

In Chapter 6 we spoke of the garment of victory breaking the power of fear. The most effective way to put on that garment of victory is by meditating on all the good things that God has done for us, those we know or those we read about in the Bible or even biographies of Godly people. As we meditate and ponder on these acts of God, we are releasing the power of testimony in our world. In Revelation 12:11 we are shown that we have the power to overcome the enemy who is called the accuser of the brethren, *'by the blood of the lamb and the word of their testimony.'* There is power in using these testimonies as we meditate, talk to others and as we pray.

In the Old Testament, many of the mighty men and women of God model effective prayer for us. They often prayed by firstly remembering God's faithfulness. Nehemiah was a man who followed God and there is a prayer written direct from his heart onto the pages of the Bible which begins with praise for the name of God.

'Arise and bless the Lord your God forever and ever! O may your glorious name be blessed and exalted above all blessing and praise!'   *Nehemiah 9:5*

Nehemiah then lists off many wonderful events and miracles that God performed for the people of Israel in the generations before him. He starts by thanking God for His faithfulness to Abraham and then Moses. He spends time remembering God's miracles and wonders and thanks Him from his heart. Then as faith grows with these ponderings, he begins to ask God for His power to change present situations.

Persistent prayer

Persistent prayer is a key tool of an overcoming and victorious life. Persistent prayer prepares your heart for bigger things. Jesus teaches his disciples to pray and keep asking for things without getting weary and wanting to give up. Every prayer we pray brings results, it's just that we don't always get to see these results immediately. Prayer is powerful and effective and we need to picture every sentence, every cry and every groan from deep in our spirits filling a bowl in heaven like incense for Jesus. In Revelation 5:8 there is a description of how our prayers shift heaven.

'The four living creatures and the twenty four elders fell down before the lamb, each one

holding a harp and golden bowls full of incense, which are the prayers of the saints.'

How incredible is that? Every second spent praying changes our lives and the lives of those around us as the things are shifted. Don't always look with your earthly eyes but be aware of the greater reality of the unseen heavenly dimension. Things always move when we pray.

Worship is a powerful weapon

On our journey towards having hearts that are prepared for success, worship is vital. It is all about being God focused and actively expressing thankfulness and love for God. There is power released when we worship and our hearts connect with the heart of God. As we worship, our hearts are filled with faith, hope and love as we forget the concerns and worries of the moment and concentrate on the beauty of God. Faith rises as our God becomes bigger again in our minds where we have previously lost reality and perspective in the struggles of life. Worshipping Jesus from our hearts brings an increase of the presence of God into our world.

Where there is more of the presence of God, there is more healing, love, mercy, and power. In the presence of God we can't help but be transformed if our hearts are hungry for Him.

The power of the Bible

The Bible is not just another book of good stories and good advice. The Bible is the word of God, and as such has extraordinary power in our lives. As we explained in Chapter 8 we can use the word of God to renew our minds, set us free, bring revelation and heal our hearts as we meditate on it. The Bible is called a sword of the Spirit which is highly effective in attacking negative thoughts and difficult situations. When I feel anxious or afraid, then I say with confidence,

'No weapon that's formed against me will prosper' Isaiah 54:17

'He that abides in the shelter of the Most High, will dwell in the shadow of the Almighty. I will say of the Lord he is my refuge and my fortress. My God in whom I trust. For it is He who delivers you from the snare of the trapper and from the deadly pestilence...' Psalm 91

All fear loses its grip as I rest in the knowledge of who God is, who I am in God and therefore how I can totally trust Him and relax.

It's vital to spend time studying the Bible, hearing God and having revelation from it. It's a powerful tool in seeing our hearts prepared for all the great things that God has for us.

Forgiving others

To understand forgiveness is a powerful key to transformation and is essential to keep our hearts in a healthy place. Jesus has a lot to teach us about forgiveness because he wants us to know freedom. In our society it has become accepted to express an inability to forgive people when they have caused great pain. Often there are news reports of people saying, 'I will never forgive them for what they have done to my loved one.' Jesus teaches us that we have to release forgiveness to people, not because they deserve it, but because if we don't then bitterness and anger grow in our hearts and seep like poison into the depths of our beings. We will not know rest in our souls but will be eaten away by feelings of misery and despair if we don't forgive those who hurt us.

'Let all bitterness and wrath and anger and clamour and slander be put away from you, along with malice. Be kind to one another, tender hearted, forgiving each other, just as God in Christ also has forgiven you.
Ephesians 4:31-32

Jesus says that He is the only judge and that we must not judge and desire revenge even when it is clear that we have been wronged. This doesn't excuse bad behaviour and we are not expected to pretend that being wronged didn't hurt. We are just asked to forgive people who hurt us because God has forgiven us.

'For if you forgive others for their transgressions, your heavenly father will also forgive you. But if you do not forgive others, then your heavenly father will not forgive your transgressions.'   *Matthew 6: 14-15*

These are serious words which we have a tendency to try and negotiate. The fact is that we have to release people in forgiveness to be judged by God alone. I picture it as if I carry these people who have hurt me around on my back until I forgive them, and then as I release them to God they are no longer weighing me down. I become free. I am aware of how much I need God to forgive me and restore me to total freedom and so I can't afford to withhold this same forgiveness from anyone else. It's not about comparison and equality, it's about loving others and being unselfish and godly in our attitudes.

Many people never know true healing in their hearts because the restoring love of God can't penetrate a hard heart which holds onto unforgiveness. This is because unforgiveness breeds anger, bitterness and rebellion which need to be dealt with in repentance. Repentance is not about feeling sorry and guilty but about making a turn around and choosing to change. We need to repent when we allow ungodly attitudes to take a hold in our lives and we need to ask for the grace of God to empower us to become more like Jesus.

It's so important to be aware of how much Jesus has forgiven us and wants to shower us with love and delight. This helps us to be free with others.

'He has not dealt with us according to our sins, nor rewarded us according to our iniquities. For as high as the heavens are above the earth, so great is His loving kindness toward those who fear him. As far as the east is from the west, so far has he removed our transgressions from us. Just as a father has compassion on his children, so the Lord has compassion on those who fear him.'

Psalm 103:10-13

Serving Others

In Isaiah 58 it explains how loving and serving others can actually speed up the healing process. This is kingdom culture which is often totally different from the worlds understanding of life! We are told that as we love and serve others we will know blessing ourselves.

'Is this not the fast that I have chosen, to lose the bonds of wickedness, to undo the bands of the yoke and to let the oppressed go free and break every yoke?
Is it not to divide your bread with the hungry and bring the homeless into your house, when you see the naked to cover him and not to hide yourself from your own flesh?
Then your light will break out like the dawn, and your recovery will speedily spring forth;

and your righteousness will go before you, the
glory of the Lord will be your rear guard.'
Isaiah 58: 6-8

We should not live our lives aimed at being successful, but should aim to be a blessing to others. That is success. As we stop the temptation to feel sorry for ourselves, and refuse to become obsessed with having our own needs met we can remain able to pour our lives out for others. God promises that as we do this we will know healing in the depths of our souls. It is an enormous privilege serving and loving others. It doesn't have to be difficult and can start with a smile! Many people are starved of love and we have the privilege of changing their lives as we begin to invest in helping them practically, taking time to talk to them, smiling at them or blessing them in some other way.

When was the last time you left some flowers on the doorstep of someone's house to spontaneously bless someone? Have you ever offered to clean the public toilets in your neighbourhood? It can be such fun to serve and bless individuals and communities as we practically demonstrate God's love for them. We have so many opportunities to bless the poor, destitute, broken, hopeless and the hard hearted. It is an enormous privilege to be Jesus hands and feet in this world where we live!

The important thing about serving others is to do it for the audience of one. We must avoid all temptation to serve other people in order to be praised or appreciated by others. Jesus criticised people in the Bible heavily for having this attitude and asks that we serve others for his affirmation only. Successful living is a life focused on others. When people become focused on personal success and their personal reputation they generally become unlike able and unpleasant to be around as they manipulate people in strategies to increase their power, status and success. People who want to be like Jesus focus on serving and loving others just as he did when he walked the earth.

Connecting to the house of God

The church is the most astounding concept which is central to living a successful, God-centred life. It is designed to be a greenhouse full of the presence of God. It is a place to give, a place to grow, a place to be connected, rooted and belong. In the house of God people find their destiny. If we build God's house by committing ourselves to serving it and helping it become a source of love, life and beauty, He builds us. We are asked to be living stones in the building of His church. A living stone can bear weight and knows that it is part of the wall. It has to connect and know its role and purpose. Peter wrote,

'...you also, as living stones, are being built up a spiritual house...'   *1 Peter 2:5*

There is power in the church because there is power in corporate worship, prayer and connecting. God designed us to be interdependent and not isolated and independent. God is passionate about his church and he wants us to be too. In order for us to be able to go on a journey to see our hearts become whole, healed and healthy we need to be part of a growing, vision filled church where the presence of God ministers to us as we minister to Him. Choosing a church is vital in the process of becoming successful, fruitful and whole. We should come to church meetings expecting to see the power of God touching people's lives, healing bodies, hearts and relationships. We should come to church meetings excited about being in the powerful presence of God and excited about experiencing his life, energy, strength and wisdom being poured into our hearts. The church meeting together is the place to go to see miracles happen and lives being restored.

Holiness

Another key to growth, breakthrough and healing is the understanding of our call as followers of Jesus, to holiness. Whilst the natural inclination for us as we seek wholeness is to become ego centred and self obsessed, Jesus asks us to be Him centred which will lead to being others centred as well. He asks us to be continually ruthless with our natural inclinations to live selfishly and 'kill our fleshly desires' as we seek His ways and His will first!

Whilst God wants to breathe life into us as His creation, in order for us to become even more free to be who we are meant to be, He also wants us to be at war with that sin which, 'so easily entangles us' and stops us knowing life in all its fullness. Holiness leads to real freedom.

Taking responsibility

An important thing to remember in our journey towards holiness and wholeness is that our emotional life is our responsibility. Our problems belong to us and no one else! We have the choices to make to find a solution for our problems and our emotional life. When we accept this responsibility we can become healed faster because we are no longer looking to others to 'sort us out'. Although other people can help us through the process of healing and clarity, ultimately we are the only ones who can initiate change and sustain it. Once I own my problem, I can look into the mirror to see who can change it with the power of God. We can be pro-active in seeking solutions by offering forgiveness, spending time in prayer, choosing to die to our natural selfish reactions, serving others, asking others for wisdom and generally having an overcoming attitude to our weaknesses.

Having Vision

It says in the Bible that *'without vision the people perish.'*(Proverbs 29:18) This is a vital key to seeing our hearts restored and prepared to see dreams fulfilled. We need to keep our eyes on the goal. Paul writes in the book of Philippians 3:14:

'I press on toward the goal ... '

We need to know that there is a purpose to our hearts journey. We need to know that there is a real reason to grasping the healing and restoration that God wants us to know. In each of us God has placed a unique dream and vision which makes our eyes sparkle and we need to keep our eyes fixed on seeing that fulfilled. If we don't know what that is then God wants to reveal it to us, so spend some time praying for revelation. The overall mission of our lives when we give ourselves to Jesus is to see His Kingdom extended and our specific dreams and visions will always be a part of that. We all have different parts to play, using our unique gifts and personalities and we need to find what our role is so that we will know true fulfilment and pleasure in achieving goals and dreams. We are called to relentlessly pursue life in all its fullness. We are expected to seize every moment of every day and squeeze from it all the life, fun, fruitfulness and influence that we can. We are called to be influencers and ambassadors for the kingdom of God! Without a clear understanding of our mission we will probably become lifeless, dry and boring, self centred people!

The value of being honest and real

At the conclusion of this book I urge you to seek wholeness so that you can know life in all its fullness. Let us be committed to being authentic and genuine about who we are without pretence, whilst seeking total healing, restoration and holiness. God wants us all to know true freedom and completeness in our identity as His children. We need to wear our garments of salvation, cloaks of victory and robes of authority and abundance as we learn to lean our hearts toward God, His will and ways. We need to continually learn to hear God's voice as louder than any one else's and walk with confidence in who we are, what we are called to do and how God views us. As we put these truths into practise, the transformation of our mess into our message will become a natural consequence!

I pray this for you as Paul prayed for us in Ephesians 3:14-21

'For this reason I bow my knees before the father, from whom every family in heaven and on earth derives its name, that He would grant you, according to the riches of His glory to be strengthened with power through his spirit in the inner man, so that Christ may dwell in your hearts through faith and that you may be rooted and grounded in love, may be able to comprehend with all the saints what is the breadth and length and height and depth, and to know the love of Christ which surpasses

knowledge, that you may be filled up to the fullness of God.

Now to Him who is able to do far more than we can ask or think, according to the power that works within us, to Him be the glory in the church and in Christ Jesus to all generations forever and ever. Amen

If anything in this book has made you feel that you need to talk to someone about the pains in your heart, then please do email the church office and we will do our best to try and put you in touch with someone to help you.

Email:
makingyourmessyourmessage@hotmail.co.uk

You might also find '**What Now? An introduction to living life with Jesus at the centre.**' a helpful book written by the same author. It is a book written to help people find a real relationship with Jesus and looks at issues such as prayer, who Jesus is, baptism, money, our thought life and others.

You can order this from Amazon, buy it at your local Christian Bookshop or order it from the church's website cccbathandbristol.com

Tools for Breakthrough